COBALT

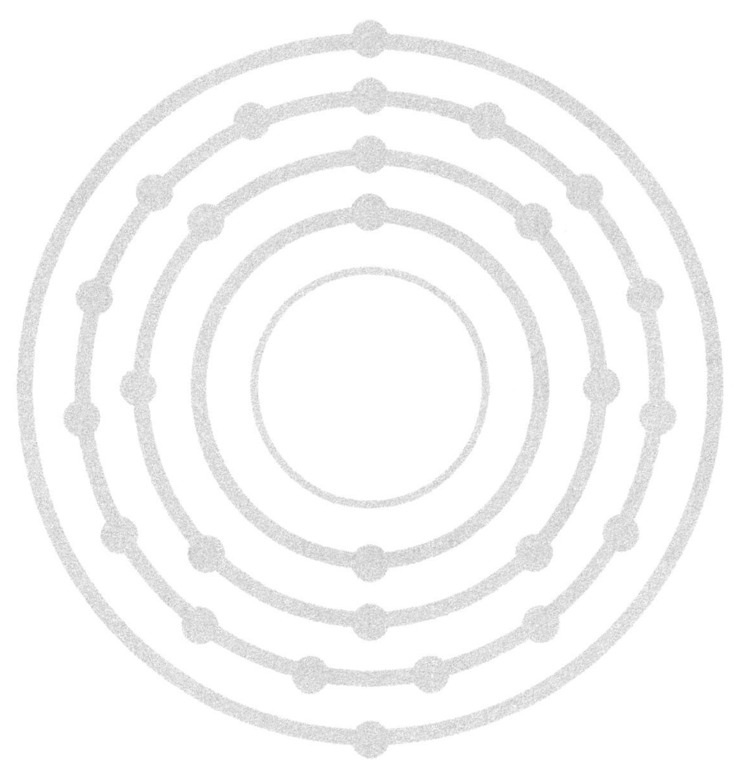

VOLUME THREE

Book design by Rachel Wooley.
Logo design by Amanda Gilleland.

Cobalt Review
Baltimore, MD

For all inquiries, please email cobalt@cobaltreview.com.

VOLUME THREE

The Staff

Baltimore, MD

www.cobaltreview.com

CONTENTS

Poetry

Author	Page	Title
Sarah Ann Winn*	1	Field Guide
Lee Ann Roripaugh	9	beautiful tsunami
Vickie Vértiz**	12	Already My Lips Were Luminous
Liz Dolan*	18	The House that Ruth Built
Jonathan Travelstead	20	Fifty-Two Hertz
Liza Porter**	45	Blue Gloves, Stars
Michael Salcman	46	That Summer Conference
Nikki Thompson**	61	Dodger Blues
Laurie Ann Guerrero**	76	Casketing
	77	Untouchable
Éireann Lorsung**	91	Kingfishers
	92	Gone
	93	Bramble
Natasha Murdock	111	The Curve of My Neck

Joseph Mills	112	Death and My Daughter: A Timeline
Ryan W. Bradley	117	This Dirty, Self-Cleaning Universe
Heather Bell	133	Last Will and Testament
Timothy Liu	149	Romance in a Red State
	150	Unsleeping, 5:03AM

Fiction

Mariana McDonald**	3	Provenance
Laura Jean Moore*	36	The Crossroads
Cara Cotter	47	The Movie Men
Anne Colwell	64	See Me
Kate Wyer	48	excerpt from *Black Krim*
Leslie Doyle	101	Red, Right, Return
Olvard Liche Smith	127	Grand Gesture
Jay Geigley**	141	After the End of the World as We Knew It: A Walkthrough
Tom Williams	155	The Last Original Guitar Riff in G

Nonfiction

Author	Page	Title
Colin Rafferty**	7	Box Score #41
Susan Rukeyser**	13	Believe It, She's Tried
Gabriel Furshong	23	Small Ball
Carrie Bistline*	72	Egress
D. Watkins	84	Class Trip
Jen McGuire	95	Falling in Love Through Van Morrison
M.C. Mah**	114	Top 10 Oakland A's Prospects
Wes Civilz**	118	exceprt from *Action: A Memoir of Lust*
Talea Anderson	135	A Guide for the Visually Impaired

Nick Hornby

28 Interview by Andrew Keating

Mary Miller

78 Interview by Andrew Keating

* 2014 Writing Prize Winner
** 2014 Writing Prize Finalist

VOLUME THREE

Sarah Ann Winn
2014 Gabriela Mistral Poetry Prize Winner

Field Guide

When there was nothing left to say, we talked about birds,
pointed out the finches' little black caps, the way
their clever claws wrap the seeds so they can pry
the husk away with their beaks. Head tilt, crack, one eye kept on us.
At the kitchen table, we looked up the ones who fluttered round our feeder.

From our corn flake field, in hedges of dishes,
we were camouflaged by cereal boxes, in a butter dish bird blind.
Besides nuthatches and chickadees, we can identify cardinals and blue jays
even in silhouette. Their peaked heads, their bully swoop to knock away
the smaller birds—the sparrows and wrens.

Our table grew still so soon after my sister died.
We hadn't yet learned to talk about birds. Our hands still shook
putting back the last plate. Newly silent. The words wouldn't come
for what's next. The silence stretched out its long neck, designed
for deep spearing, always ready to stand in the water, to be patient, calm.

To becalm. My grandmother found the blue crane. Sketched
in long grey lines and deliberate stasis on our dock or across
the lake, water-doubled, angled through water lilies.
Come winter, ducks shivered around the small open patch
of ice near the spillway. The always present birds. We have the birds,

always. Like them, we forgot, for a while, how to go to warmer places.
We keep the birdhouse full, the feeder regularly checked,
lid raised and lowered, manual grain elevator, we think
about the birds as instructed. Someone has told us
to avoid millet, and who knew how popular peanuts would be.

We consider the sparrows. We weigh thistle and sunflower.
We try to count the goldfinches when they gather and spar.
More than ten, maybe many more, maybe fifty
flying in and out of the barbary hedge
to fight by the feeder filled over and over.

I want to multiply my hours this way,
account for what's flown into branches, only half seen,
count the minutes who move too quickly twice.
Sit at the kitchen table, stand endlessly drying dishes.
Search the grey sky for signs of peregrination.
Stay around the feeder, keep hunger at bay.

Mariana McDonald
2014 Zora Neale Hurston Fiction Prize Finalist

Provenance

She asked where it was from.

The puzzled seller wasn't sure what the question meant.

"You mean where was it made? I'm not quite sure."

She answered simply then: "Where did you get it?" She was thinking just one word: provenance.

She had noted the garnet ring on Kitschy months before, and put it in her *favorites*. From time to time, she clicked on its image and marveled at its design: a ring with a faceted garnet held by prongs in a slim gold setting. Elegant, simple, beautiful.

Just like hers.

The garnet ring her parents gave her. She could not remember when. Just that she'd had it for many years before the day it disappeared. Stolen.

•

They were living in a second-story flat in Dorchester, the one with the dizzying wallpaper, that they had marched their boxes to, when they were evicted from a place down the street for making too much noise.

The flat was big enough, and moving so close kept them in the neighborhood, with the same bus stops and wash-and-dry. The new landlord wouldn't care about noise. He was never to be seen, a fact they enjoyed until the Boston night when the heater went dead and there was no one to fix it. They called around to friends to see where they could stay, packing the cats in a crate for the trip.

That was how they were. Always figuring out things together, calming each other down as they hashed out solutions.

"We'll freeze to death if we stay here," she said.

"I bet we can stay at Jaime's place," he offered. "He's still in Arecibo. We just need to get a key."

They made it through that time with calm. It was something he always had in good supply, it seemed, and a reason she was drawn to him.

One evening in the kitchen when they were first seeing each other, she opened the trash can to drop in bits of unused vegetables. She screamed when she saw a small army of maggots making their way out the side of the bin.

"It's ok," he said calmly as he quickly gathered and closed up the trash bag, capturing all the slimy trekkers, and whisked it off out the door. She fell in love with him then and there.

It was no wonder he could be calm in the face of maggots. He had seen so much more. He grew up in poverty on the island, in Mayagüez, working odd jobs from the age of six. When his father died mysteriously and they were thrown off the hacienda he was only eight, and from then on he worked day and night shining shoes, sweeping floors, whatever he could do to bring home a bit of bread. They called it *matahambre*—something to kill the hunger.

But he was never bitter. All the things that could have worn down a lesser person just seemed to make him sweeter, stronger, more understanding. Even the drugs were like that, or rather, his addiction.

It started in New York City, when he was a teenager. They had been forced to take the air shuttle to Nueva Yol when the island seemed to tell them there was nothing left.

It wasn't just one thing that made it happen. There were many. The angrily-spat-out epithets that only saw his dark skin and heard his accent. The working conditions in factories full of poisons. The pain of missing the countryside, the sights and sounds and smells of his beloved country. The birth injury of his daughter that no one seemed able to heal.

But the worst thing was the death of his son in a tenement fire.

These things were all thieves, taking piece after piece of his hope, his pride, and his manhood.

In the midst of this turgid sea, street-corner thugs making a living threw out what seemed like a lifesaver: Smack. Horse. Dope. Heroin.

He caught the lifesaver in his arms, and it took over his whole body, his life. It made for slammed doors of family members, wanting no tecato to come and steal what little they had.

Those were terrible years of isolation, violence, and jail.

When his beloved mother took her last breaths, he tossed down the glove, determined to end it, make something of his life, fight whatever way he could for his country.

That was years ago, long before they met. Today he was an activist and a drug counselor, helping other lost young men and women find a way out of the trap he'd been in.

So when his nephew Federico asked for a place to stay in Boston, a place to regroup as he quit drugs, he did not slam the door on him. He welcomed Fede into the apartment with the dizzying wallpaper and told him he was home.

He knew such kindness was a blessing for Fede. At the same time, he let himself forget all the bad things he himself had done when he was a junkie, things he did not want to remember. Things that justified slammed doors, his family just trying to protect themselves.

"Fede, can you get me the tin of coffee from the top shelf?" she called out to her nephew. "I'm going to make some breakfast."

She thought she'd heard Fede stirring a while ago as she slept in. Thought she heard him rustling about the apartment, already awake.

He didn't answer. She tied her robe about her and put on her slippers. As she walked to the extra bedroom she felt a stab of cold in her shoulders.

Fede's bed was unmade, sheets crumpled to one side, the heavy blanket sliding off the edge of the bed. Fede's backpack was not in the spot where it normally rested, surrounded by his socks and sneakers and dirty underwear. They were all gone.

"Cariño, wake up!" she called out as she rushed to the bedroom. "Fede's gone."

They looked around to see if Fede had left a note, some word of where he was going and for how long. Maybe he was looking for a job, decided to take his dirty clothes to the wash-and-dry.

Nothing.

Then she felt a shiver of worry that made her feel ashamed.

"Do you think…?" she uttered as she walked back to the room where Fede was staying, to check the small box they kept out of sight in the closet. It was on the top shelf. She grabbed a stool to reach it. As she went to grab it, her hand was surprised, like when one goes to shake someone's hand and they hold it back and suddenly one is reaching for nothing.

The box was pushed to the back of the shelf. Empty.

She gasped. All their cash—not much, but all that they had—was gone. His leather and silver bolo with the turquoise arrowhead. The collection of change they hoped would grow into something. And the most valuable item: a gold garnet ring from her parents.

•

They never heard a word from him. Fede just disappeared. Family said Fede had gone to Worcester or Framingham or maybe New York. No one was sure.

It was only years later they heard he was gone for good, dead from the disease, from SIDA, just like his two brothers and a cousin.

All of them now what was called “IVDUs” in the talk of painful acronyms. Intravenous drug users. Needle-sharers. Junkies. Tecatos.

•

The garnet ring on Kitschy startled her.

It was decades since that awful morning discovery, and she was now a widow.

She window-shopped on Kitschy and other such sites, from time to time buying something for herself or buying materials for her jewelry-making business.

Sometimes she would search “gold garnet ring.”

These searches most often yielded fancy-looking rings swaddled in diamonds or other gems that she thought lacked imagination.

But this one was the spitting image of the one that had been stolen.

So asking where the seller got it made sense.

But what in fact would she do, could she do, if the buyer said, “I picked this up in a pawn shop in Boston years ago”?

It was with great relief that she read the seller’s answer: “This ring was my own, from my childhood in Ontario.”

“I now live in Los Angeles,” the seller added. “I have just a few of my own personal items that I’m selling, along with those I’ve collected.”

She did the mental calculations. One could buy a ring from a pawn shop in Boston and then travel to Canada to sell it there. And it could be bought by someone looking for a bargain ring to give to a daughter, who later sold it, and....

Right, she thought. Enough.

And then, suddenly, she knew that what she wanted was not the ring. Not the elegant curve of gold, the firm hold of prongs, the flash of garnet.

What she really wanted was Fede’s innocence.

She wanted the innocence of a young man making his way in life, unmarred by crime or addiction, not yet damaged by the ways of the world. And she wanted his innocence of the crime itself.

She wanted his appreciation and affection and she wanted him alive. She wanted to hear him say,

“Sure, Tia! I’ll get it down for you. Can we have pancakes?”

Colin Rafferty
2014 Earl Weaver Baseball Writing Prize Finalist

Box Score (#41)

He is left-handed, perfect for first base, the edge of his foot on the bag while he stretches out his lanky frame for the ball that comes to him from the infield. When his Yale teammates throw, it is perfect, Ivy League quality, a searing bit of whiteness that does not lazily arc through the sky but rather buzzes, high-pitched, an angry insect that the flytrap of his glove will close upon. It is perfect for him to use his body this way, this clean movement of muscle. When he was a pilot in the war, he bailed out of a burning airplane, his parachute jerking his body as he fell to Earth. This is better, to use his body this way.

It is 1990. The war gets farther away every day. He played in the first two College World Series, although Yale lost both times. Part of his job now is to throw out a first pitch every year, to open the season officially; Taft started this, with his corpulence so different from George's own body. George is a sportsman; the body doesn't forget. But he was a first baseman, not a pitcher; he is used to collecting the ball, not throwing it, the double play ends with him, Tinker to Evans to Bush.

He throws out a first pitch in Canada this year, at the new stadium. He meets with their Prime Minister, for talks (their official reason), but he is there for the baseball, for the chance to be on the field again.

He wears a Texas Rangers jacket, the team his son owns. He grins broadly when stepping onto the field, lighter and happier than his Canadian counterpart. He points to his catcher, calling the pitch, snaps it off while the Prime Minister is setting himself. The form is still there, the drawing back, the following through, the ball leaving his hand as simply and cleanly as the SkyDome's retractable roof (which is not retracted).

How little time remains for George to do this. Just twice more before he is called out, retired by the rookie from Arkansas. It's a pitcher/first baseman play, to try to pick off the runner on first. Caught him napping, the announcers say.

But that day in Toronto, under the roof, all that is far ahead of him. George is pure joy at this moment, an old man at the top of his game, a young man remembering his game. As they interview him in a suite later, the crowd will roar at the action on the field. He'll hear it, crook his thumb over his shoulder towards the noise; I like all that, he'll say, the grin again.

Lee Ann Roripaugh

beautiful tsunami

it's no secret she's a little bit vain

vain in the way reptiles are vain

a 10-story building's worth of solipsism

with her head full of snakes
that paralytic stare

coconut palms and mangroves tricked up
along the shoreline don't slow her down

sea walls can't stop her

labyrinths of floodgates won't fool her
into siphoning away her power

she's a mega-tsunami of pure hubris
cross-dressed in high femme
splashy / shiny / crystalline
all liquid curve and fluid light

with her hello kitty barrettes
pink glitter ribbons furbelowing
all that snaky girlzilla hair

bored now, she pouts in her little girl voice
before it all goes to shit

RAAAHRRR!!! she hollers

SKREEEEEE!!! she thrashes her tail

HRRRRRRR… she thrums pensively

bullets and fireballs and even atomic blasts
can't stop her

she wants to smash it all to bits
easy-peasy as a spurned lover
sweeping cutlery and crockery
off the restaurant table

the brilliantine petulant clatter of it

fuck the puny villagers
with their tiny flaming matchsticks !

fuck the helicopters she swats
away like lethargic flies !

fuck those candy-shelled tanks
the marching termite armies !

send in the smog monster !

summon mothra !

bring on ghidorah !

as if / the mirror stage
of her own monstrosity

might make her recoil

call in the mecha-tsunami !

as if / the feedback loop
of her cyborg doppelganger
might give her pause

when instead:

she surfaces like a terrible fish

rises like the Dark Phoenix

comes in for the kiss like Narcissus

ardent to drown
in the exquisitely bruised splendor
of her face

Vickie Vértiz
2014 Gabriela Mistral Poetry Prize Finalist

Already My Lips Were Luminous

after "Any People" by Else Lasker-Schuler

My first kiss is with an uncle
comforting
me as Mom throws
up two dollar wine

I do not know the language
Sitting on the edge of a faded red plastic couch
Grateful in an ill-fitting girl dress lavender roses dot the chest
The embrace is short His breath cases of cigarettes and one aluminum beer
He says good night, the songs
of crows outside unspool

When his sons leave for the Persian Gulf he kisses them too
and I'm confused
because men never embrace around me they shove each other's oil hands into
car guts and machines that make glass not tender not soft

I understand now there must be other ways to love
your children
For the me in the dress, I long for her
a dream where she doesn't have to pretend
to be innocent

Susan Rukeyser
2014 Frank McCourt Creative Nonfiction Prize Finalist

Believe It, She's Tried

In 1995, I probably could have published my first novel, *Landings*. But I didn't. For the next ten years I wrote almost nothing. Telling this story means explaining the cluster of years that diverted me, those three years when I lost a marriage, a literary agent, and a job.

The job wasn't such a big deal. The other stuff, yes. I'm not sure I want to tell this story.

Not all those who wander are lost[1]

I have a ceramic plaque engraved with this because I want to be one of those deliberate wanderers. In the years immediately following college in New York, I breezily relocated to San Francisco, then Seattle, then England's blustery north to start my Creative Writing MA. Wanderers want to go everywhere, try everything. We split off from broad paths and scurry down game trails, only to be outsmarted by prey we come to realize we don't really want. We bushwhack wilderness to unexpected joy. Or a mess of thorns and poison sumac, we can't know until we try. We breathe in experience.[2] We lose track of time. Some of us are staggered by heartbreak.

As of this writing, I haven't published *Landings*, or any book, but I still call myself a writer. I write every day: stories, poems, essays. I complete things. I lose myself in words, agonize over them, exalt in every finished piece, no matter how tiny. In journals, I publish short work I'm proud to share. For some, my work resonates. That's success. Truly, that's happiness! We must rejoice in doing what we we're best at, what revs our engines and makes sense. We must celebrate doing, not just achieving.

That's all I have to say about that.[3]

In 1993, I married the wrong man. It happens. I didn't know he was wrong. Or, I didn't believe. A year later, *Forrest Gump* convinced me. Let me explain.

I thought it was strange that my husband wanted to see *Forrest Gump*, or any movie, when we reunited after a move to England, weeks apart.

Stranger still that he insisted, even when I told him I'd already seen it. Yes, Forrest Gump was a red flag. I only knew that later. We went to town and were silent together in the dark. Days later, I began my Creative Writing MA at Lancaster University. I never saw my husband again.

Lancaster is a charming old cathedral city full of interesting people. You get used to the smell of sheep. The grey skies were harder for me, especially with the bewildering turn my life had taken. Peacocks, gifted to the University by a lesser royal, I think someone said, strutted back and forth across the campus. They regularly passed beneath my dorm room window, sending up doleful, lusty shrieks. Next door, my suitemate elicited a similar response from his pretty girlfriend. It was to these sounds that I wrote *Landings*. I was reeling, in suspended shock. My life had veered off course, very far from home and quite without my consent. Suddenly, I didn't feel like a wanderer; I just felt lost. So I wrote, obsessively, the only action I knew how to accomplish. I tapped out chapter after chapter on the Mac Classic I'd hauled from Seattle and across an ocean.

One of my professors insisted that writing composed on a computer was inauthentic. He was suspicious of me anyway, believing Americans spoiled and greedy. He thought my writing was sentimental and awkward. I suspect that's what he thought of me. His generalizations gave me reason to doubt his judgment, however. I threw myself into the work. I'd never experienced anything like it and I was hooked: the chapters rose before me, one after the other, fully outlined. The characters whispered their secrets, yanked me along to the conclusion.

I finished and revised *Landings*, and short stories, and poems. Creatively, I'd never been so fertile. Personally, I was barren and depleted. My periods ceased. I became too strict about diet and exercise, as some of us do, controlling what we can. I played the role of a functioning human being, but every moment was a lie. At night I lay stiff as anxiety smothered, pinned me to the thin dorm mattress.

...if you will, please let me elicit support for *Landings*.[4]

Returning to Connecticut, where I was raised, I signed with a literary agent. It happened easily. I know exactly how easily because I recently tried again, to no avail. Back then, agents were queried by mail only. There was email but not the internet, not like today. There were still a number of big publishers, not yet reduced to a handful of conglomerates. Agents didn't seem so utterly hopeless about debut literary fiction.

My agent worked for a New York City agency that still exists, although she's no longer there. She was excited about me and my book. She gave me hope. I hadn't had that for a while. Her agency was best known for its authors of celebrity biographies. Another red flag I ignored. But I figured, surely she knew better than I, what to do with this book? This was good news, wasn't it? After so much lousy? I'd do anything to keep that hope.

Six months and a few submissions to big publishers later, she dropped me. Even though one respected HarperCollins editor liked it and wrote a kind letter before sending it "up the chain." That second editor ultimately declined, sending a letter that praised my talents but fretted about projected sales. Some might take this as an encouraging sign, to get even this far with Harper. They might see this as an indication that *Landings* could almost certainly find a home somewhere, maybe a much smaller house.

My agent dumped me. Not kindly. She sent a terrible letter I've kept to this day. I know, I know. Should've tossed it.

Coming on the heels of that other, worse, divorce, I finally let despair flood me, a leaky dam burst. My words were gone. Scattered and drowned, I assumed. For the next few years I recovered. I got a job (and lost it). I opened a used bookstore (and closed it). Then I had a baby.

No purpose had more clearly presented itself to me than motherhood. This glorious creature needed everything from me, and to my surprise I found I had everything to give, and more. It was as if some part of me remembered motherhood, this naturally consuming joy.

Landings was in a box in a closet. I didn't even have a Mac anymore, or any way to read my old floppy discs. A dream was dead, but look what I had instead! Unencumbered by writing and all the emotion associated with it, I was able to give my full attention to my baby as he became a happy, curious child. More years passed without words, and most of the time I didn't miss them. Writing was another lost love I learned to live without.

Until I couldn't, not for one more day.

It's just change. It's just time shoving us all forward, on to the next.[5]
My words returned in New Jersey. Another flood, but this one of images and ideas and that gut-gnawing need to tell a story, to send words out into the universe in hope of connection. One day I just started to dream a new novel, what ultimately became *Not on Fire, Only Dying*. Every moment I wasn't working or parenting, I mapped plot points, visualized characters, setting. Finally, after moving to Texas, I set to putting it down on paper. I was relieved to discover the characters had waited for me. They still wanted me to tell their stories. I finished the novel, revised and revised, and finally started querying agents. A gratifying number requested to see the full manuscript, but in the end all said no. My writing was good, they said, my characters and story intriguing, but they weren't sure about the multiple perspectives. And maybe there was too much exposition? I withdrew it from consideration, and after yet another move—yes, a

wanderer, still!—I started over. I rewrote the novel, sentence by sentence. Without any assurance of a different response from agents, I did it because it was artistically necessary, as every writer must be willing to do. I studied those rejection letters: Did I see patterns in the complaints? What did I need to change, and what did I stand behind?

I rewrote the novel from only one character's point of view. I had to admit, it was better. And tighter, by a whopping 20,000 words. *Now* it was ready, surely? This time, agents were again kind and encouraging when they declined representation. My writing was good and my characters and story intriguing, but did I know how hard it was to publish fiction these days? Especially a small literary novel by an unknown? Some said it was too gritty (drugs, sex, mental illness); others said it was too sweet (a love story is at its core). It was too far outside the mainstream, or it was too conventional. One agent said my writing felt aloof, as if I'd thrust out an arm between us. Now that might be fair. Sometimes that might be me..

An alloy has been added. Now he will crack along different lines when tapped. [6]

There is a scene in the movie *Poltergeist* where JoBeth Williams stands at one end of a long hallway. At the other end is the door to her children's room, aglow with bad magic. She runs toward it, but the hallway stretches longer and the door pulls further and further away. Her instinct and stubbornness finally override this trick, and she pushes through and reaches the door. I picture this scene when I think of where I am now with my writing. For too long it felt as if my goals moved further and further out of reach. My momentum was cut by criticism I took in too deeply. I surrendered to self-doubt. Now I'm pushing through. I'm running for my life.

I shouldn't have quit writing. I should've found another agent, or queried small publishers directly. I should have maintained the pace I set at Lancaster. Maybe you would have known this, and saved yourself my trouble? I know there are writers who do, and I admire them. All we can do is our best, and sometimes that falls short of what we *should* do. Some years melt you down. Then all you can do is take time to reconstruct. Build yourself stronger, and, yes, a little harder, so the new foundation will hold.

At 46, my voice is seasoned by hurt, as many are. It is mine, authentic, although I still compose on a computer, like that professor said I shouldn't. I won't stop writing again, not for any reason. I'm not naïve or suffering delusions of grandeur. Not bitter. Well maybe a little bitter, sometimes. I don't ignore red flags.

Now and then, sure, I feel that feathery panic: I'm too late. I missed my chance. But I try to trust this path I'm on, the one that led me to the wrong man and the wrong agent but also to my present life, with the right man, and my extraordinary son, and the frenzied, creative productivity of a writer at mid-life, watching the clock.

Art is not a thing, it is a way[7]

I hope *Not on Fire, Only Dying* finds a home. I'd be thrilled to meet a publisher who believes in it, someone who's comfortable with gritty, marginalized characters and their sweet love story. Who trusts me as storyteller.

In the meantime, I write. I publish a variety of short work, exploring format and style and subject, while purging the stories clogging my brain. I write to process thoughts. To escape, to belong, all of that. Everything is different from how I expected it to be. It's so much better.

Maybe, as I head toward 50, I'll smarten up and finally write a third novel, and a fourth, and maybe another cluster of years will divert me, this time in good ways. For now, success is knowing I create work that says what I mean. Success is knowing some of you understand completely. It's connecting with the world through words.

We wanderers must go at whatever pace feels right. So what if we miss some deadlines we set for ourselves when we were too young to know better? Let's tell our stories, even when we're not sure we want to. Let's believe the path is the destination.

---

[1] From the poem "All that is gold does not glitter," by J.R.R. Tolkien, *The Fellowship of the Ring*

[2] References a line from "Poem Out of Childhood" by Muriel Rukeyser

[3] Dialogue from *Forrest Gump*

[4] From a letter to me from Larry Ashmead, HarperCollins editor, dated 10/5/95

[5] Dialogue from my forthcoming novel, *Not on Fire, Only Dying*

[6] From "The Unjustly Punished Child" by Sharon Olds

[7] Quote by Elbert Hubbard

Liz Dolan
2014 Earl Weaver Baseball Writing Prize Winner

The House that Ruth Built

In front of a hole in the right field wall
my father spreads the tarpaulin to protect
the grounds from a sudden downpour.

His once slender waist now bulges like
the Babe's, too many center-cut pork chops
and home-grown spuds. On his forearm, a tattoo,

Hands Across the Sea, two hands shaking
over the red, white and blue, the green, white
and gold, a tryst between Ireland and America.

With a North-Irish brogue, he'd tell us
they lament the loss of the old country
where they hadn't a flute to jig to,

this is the greatest country in the world
and don't you forget it.
As if forgetting how he'd gotten these afternoons

at the stadium: the truck owner, a well-connected Yank,
one hand washing the other, I guess, who bestowed
that job upon him after its wheels crushed

his five-year-old son's head, a job he kept
through the Golden Age of Baseball
'til the New York, New Haven and Hartford,

a pensioned position, beckoned. In lieu of his son's blues
he saw Lou Gehrig's weep, his cracking voice
bouncing off the bleachers and DiMaggio's velvets

squint in the two o'clock sun, his hand sheltering them
as though he were saluting. At home,
thirty blocks south, we baked scones to the tattoo of the kettle

and the drone of Mel Allen's loamy *Going, going, gone.*

Jonathan Travelstead

Forthcoming from *How We Bury Our Dead*, Cobalt Press

Fifty-Two Hertz

"Imagine roaming the world's largest ocean year after year alone, calling out with the regularity of a metronome and hearing no response...the animal is saying, 'I'm out here'...but nobody is phoning home."
—Andrew Revkin, *The New York Times*

Marine biologists listen
through their underwater instruments
to this solitary baleen whale
and name her for her song's
unique frequency,

an exhausted cry no other whales can hear.

•

So we call her June,
give her a human name,
claim her as if we could erase her loneliness
the way we erase our own:

erecting antennae, slinging radio waves
like ships that sail beyond the script
on the map's border that reads
here be dragons,

hoping a postcard with a bit of code that says

You are

comes lobbing back to our wide, gray dishes.
Does not.

So we call ourselves billions
                                                  of ones and zeroes
exiting a hole,
falling from a scarp's blasted entrance
to slate-bruised knees
                                        where we pray for a story
we can believe.

•

Or we pray for rain to fall as snakes
                that bite their tails in prairie grass
and roll to the horizon

                where dust-browned leaves rise in a conjured gale.

Or we pray for tufts of nebulae
                that shake glimmering dust from their locks,
christen our foreheads with soot.

                Holding out for a switch flicked in the heavens,
we pray for confirmation.

•

June, what if your song returns from a distant place?

•

An alien haunted my bedside as a child.
Its almond head,
the ink-black ovals that passed for its eyes
paralyzed
me in them,
one brackwater finger
held to its subtraction sign mouth
took from me the knowledge I was alone.

•

June, let us each come forward
and join the swelling solitudes.
Let us commune
in this dark's first burning breath
and experience
the stars' frequencies
individual in light and sound,

each unique as the fingerprint's gentle sine

shining their celestial voices down on us.
May we not refuse their beauty
which says
I see you. I name you.

Gabriel Furshong

Small Ball

Tickets were just a couple dollars when Mary Gunstone started attending Helena Brewers baseball games in 1985, but she got her first one for free. It was Buttrey's Food and Drug night at the ballpark and employees were given complimentary tickets. Mary was a baker at the store and also served as the staff photographer. She took her camera to that first game, started snapping photos of the players and never stopped.

In three decades since then, Mary has only missed two games: the first for her father's funeral and the second for her 50th class reunion. "I told 'em they should have it at the ballpark, but they didn't do that for me," she says, with a touch of regret.

Her commitment, especially at this lowest level of minor league baseball, has not gone unnoticed. "It seems like every ballpark has some fan or special story about a fan who frequents those games," says Paul Fetz, general manager of the Brewers. "But I've never, in my 25 years in the game, encountered a fan who does what she does, the effort she puts forward for these players."

•

Across the country, there are over 200 minor league teams associated with Major League Baseball (MLB), from Los Angeles, CA, to Danville, VA, and as the list of cities descends from large to small, there is a reverse correlation between the celebrity of the game and the intimacy of the experience. Helena, Montana (pop. 28,190), lies at the bottom of that list, among the top-ten smallest markets in all of professional baseball. To find a tinier professional baseball town, you'd have to prowl the backwoods of West Virginia.

Since 1978, Helena has hosted a team in the Pioneer League, an advanced rookie league with eight teams located five rungs down the ladder from the MLB. In the Pioneer League, games are played without the major league distractions of six and seven figure salaries or the 24-hour sports media. This is especially true in Helena, where the worst seat at

Kindrick Legion Field is only 100 feet from a professional ball player and players are still housed by the fans, so you can take one home if you have a spare bed.

Here, ninety percent of the tickets go for less than $8 and game-day availability is never a problem; attendance in 2012 was just 880 fans per game, a third of the league average. Mary Gunstone, however, is one fan the Brewers have learned to count on.

When Buttrey's Food and Drug closed down in 2008, Mary was forced to retire after 37 years with the store. She now lives on a pension and spends roughly $3,000 of her fixed income each year to print a small photo album for every player as a season-ending gift. She brought two of the albums to a Brewers playoff game last fall in a plastic grocery bag.

Seated in the stands, her toes barely touched the ground. At 71 years old, her short stature and round frame project a matronly appearance, and her tendency to finish sentences with a self-amused giggle only enhances the image of a good-natured grandmother.

"The summer I first started I would just take different pictures and give them to 'em," she explained with a quiet laugh. "Well, that didn't work out too well because some players would get hurt because they didn't get one, so I decided I'd better give all the players one."

Each page of the two albums, from the '89 and '95 seasons, contained a portrait of a player in the locker room or on the field. On the last pages were portraits of Mary herself, standing tall and wearing a proud smile.

"If I'm not here then they ask where I'm at!" she said, looking up from the pages. "I feel like I belong to the team."

•

By mid-September last year, Mary's team had completed an impressive run to a 10th league championship berth in 36 years. They were knotted at one game apiece in a three-game series to the Idaho Falls Chukars, an affiliate of the Kansas City Royals. The rubber match was scheduled for September 16th at Kindrick Legion Field.

The morning dawned dreary and cold. Mary hadn't missed a game all season and despite the bad weather, she arrived at the park an hour early. By the third or fourth inning, the gravel parking area, wedged between a Coca-Cola distribution center and the third base bleachers, would be filled with the voices of grade-school boys zigzagging between parked cars in pursuit of foul balls. But an hour before game time, it was just beginning to fill.

"Bengal" Bill sat on a stool selling programs just inside the gate. A victim of bad knees, the longtime Brewers employee was once well-known for his breathless “Gimme a B!” chants, which went on to spell either Bengals or Brewers depending on whether he was cheering for the high school basketball team or the local baseball club.

From Bengal Bill’s domain in the modest concession area, a short tunnel leads underneath the 82-year-old wooden grandstand, which faces southwest. The orientation is unique for a professional baseball stadium because it places the setting sun directly in the eyes of a right-handed hitter. The trade-off is what Fetz calls “one of the best views in all of baseball.” Emerging from the tunnel, fans are treated to an unbroken vista of rambling, forested ridgelines that sweep eastward from the mile-high summit of Mount Helena, a 620-acre city park in right center field, to Mount Ascension beyond the left field foul line.

The view however, was fleeting on this chilly September evening. Low clouds were settling on the peaks and the temperature was hovering at 50 degrees. A thunderstorm had rolled through town earlier in the afternoon and a young man in a Brewers jacket and cap was hastily toweling off seats in the front row. Fetz stood nearby surveying the crowd, wondering whether the threat of further rain would keep people away. Only a sprinkling of fans populated the stands.

Mary looked a bit worried as well. She had perched herself on a metal folding chair in her usual pre-game spot just above the home dugout, nose-to-nose with the safety netting behind home plate. As always, she wore a Milwaukee Brewers warm up jacket and a Helena Brewers ball cap, which seemed to float on top of her curly grey hair.

“Every time they win a championship, they’re always out of town,” she explained. “And I told ‘em once that I’d like to see it done here.” Sitting on the edge of her seat, fidgeting with her camera lens, she was the picture of a fretful parent as the players began their warm up tosses.

It was easy to see why her maternal instincts were triggered. A review of the 35-man roster revealed an average age of 23 years and while a major league payday may be in store for a few of them, their chances of playing even one game in the big leagues hovers around seven percent. For now, they’re just kids making less than minimum wage, wondering whether they’ll need to find a second job in the off-season.

“I’ve lived in Helena all my life and never married so I adopt these kids all summer,” Mary said. “This is my family here, the kids I call ‘em.”

•

It was a few minutes before the first pitch at 7:05PM and fans were flowing into the park steadily now, most with blankets under their arms. The sun had dipped below the Continental Divide to the west and a low fog engulfed the lights, creating four dewy halos above the outfield grass. The temperature was 48 degrees at first pitch and fans could see their breath as they settled into orange plastic seats, recycled from the Oakland Coliseum and still marked with the green and yellow Athletics logo.

The pitching matchup appeared to favor the Brewers with third round draft pick Barrett Astin on the mound who had a 1.79 ERA over 18 appearances with the Arkansas Razorbacks in the spring. He squeaked through the first three innings despite putting three runners in scoring position, but a 0-0 tie was broken in the top of the fourth after an error, a walk, and a three-run homer to the Chukars catcher, Frank Schwindel.

The Brewers went down one-two-three in the bottom half of the inning but managed to load the bases in the fifth after a single and two hit batsman. Seven members of the local booster club held letters up for the crowd. "Gimme a B!" they shouted. The crowd responded enthusiastically as Michael Ratteree, the Pioneer League MVP, stepped up to the plate.

Batting .314 with 12 home runs, Ratteree was exactly the person the Brewers wanted in this situation. "What's that spell!" the boosters screamed. "Louder!"

The ball jumped off Ratteree's bat just like it had all season. Over a thousand plastic seats snapped shut as fans took to their feet. It looked like a no-doubter, but the ball died on the warning track and fans fell back into their seats with a collective groan.

The Chukars tacked on three more runs in the next two innings. The score was 6-0 when the PA announcer began leading a disheartened crowd in a chorus of "Take Me Out to the Ballgame." Most of the boosters were singing despite the shutout, but Mary sat silently at the end of her row.

"Oh, I'm so sad I could just cry," she said. Tears had welled up in her eyes. "They're just giving it to 'em," she exclaimed, slapping her knees with both palms. "But I have to support 'em anyway."

Nearby, the boosters had arrived at the same conclusion. They pulled out their letters for one last cheer, but bad luck on the field had apparently spread to the stands. A young woman holding the *S* was clearly misplaced between the *W* and the *E*. Several fans tried to alert her to the error, but their directions were drowned out by the boosters' booming voices.

It took only 20 more minutes for the season to end and even less for 1,500 people to clear out of the tiny ballpark. By the time the trophy was presented to the Chukars manager there was only a sprinkling of dejected fans left and Mary sat among them.

•

The following spring arrived late after a long winter that dumped heavy snowfall in almost every mountain range across Montana. The gates of Kindrick Legion opened for the season's first game at 6PM on June 16th in a light but steady rain. The temperature gauge rested at a familiar 50 degrees.

Mary was already at her post, hovering above the home dugout in a navy blue poncho that covered her head-to-toe. She leaned on the handles of a walker and when she turned I could see plastic tubes resting under her nose, leading to a green oxygen tank at her feet.

"I had two cataract surgeries in March and got pneumonia in April," she explained with a ragged voice. "One doctor sent me to another doctor and finally I said, 'You've gotta get me healthy. Baseball season is coming!'" Though her cheeks were sunken, her smile was just as warm as it had been the season before.

At 7PM, Fetz strode on the field with a microphone. Rain dampened his shoulders as he held an open hand to the heavens. "Well, fans, not the best baseball weather tonight, but you're here and that's what matters, right?" A smattering of applause lifted from the seats and several fans whistled their affirmation.

The Brewers picked up where they left off nine months earlier; by the seventh inning stretch, the Missoula Osprey, a Diamondbacks affiliate, were leading eight to two. The drizzle had grown into a steady rain and Mary had abandoned her folding chair to seek shelter under the roof of the grandstand.

As we sat down for the bottom half of the inning, I noticed a silver ball-and-glove pendant on her cap. "That was a gift from Tristan's parents," she explained, removing her hat to see the pendant for herself.

Tristan Archer was a right-handed pitcher who threw 38 innings with the Brewers the previous year. Mary met his parents at Kindrick Legion one evening early in the summer. She took pictures of the young man all summer and gave them to him to share with his parents. Late in the season, a card arrived to the ballpark addressed to the "photographer lady." The pendant was tucked inside with a note from Tristan's parents: *Thanks for all the photos of Tristan. He sure loves you.*

Tristan finished the season with a respectable 3.08 ERA and earned a promotion to Single-A in Appelton, Wisconsin. It's unlikely that Mary will ever see him again but she wore the pendant proudly as she looked out onto a rain-soaked field full of new faces. Out of a 32-man roster, only two men had played in Helena the previous year.

"They don't know me yet," she said, chasing the sentence with her characteristic giggle. "But they will."

Nick Hornby:
The *Cobalt* Interview

Nick Hornby is the author of the novels *Slam, High Fidelity, About a Boy* and *A Long Way Down,* as well a book on his life as a devoted supporter of Arsenal Football Club, *Fever Pitch.* Hornby recently adapted Cheryl Strayed's *Wild* for the screen, and his latest novel is *Funny Girl.*
He lives in North London.

by Andrew Keating

Nick Hornby
The *Cobalt* Interview

Andrew Keating: Since it was such a fun topic in last year's issue (Victor LaValle, author of *The Devil in Silver*), I'd like to start by asking how music has influenced your writing, particularly in your early work. Certainly, *High Fidelity* is packed with music-loving goodness, and *Juliet, Naked* chronicles the pains of lifelong rock-god fandom. What fuels your love of music, and how do you bring that to your writing?

Nick Hornby: I don't think anything fuels my love of music—I just love music, and have always loved it. But my love of music fuels my writing, definitely. Melody lines, chord changes, harmonies, rhythm, solos…I want the feelings that you get from the best of those elements in everything I write. And I quite often respond as a listener, rather than a reader, to other people's books. When I first read Cheryl Strayed's *Wild*, which I then adapted for a movie, I heard Springsteen's 1978 live shows in there—the anger, the commitment, the sincerity, the redemption. *Juliet, Naked* was about a musician, but it was supposed to be about the way we consume art, any art—it's just that musicians are much more fun to write about than, say, writers—and music fans are more fun to write about than literary devotees.

AK: As a sort of cyclical follow-up, tell me about your relationship with Ben Folds, with whom you put together the album *Lonely Avenue*. How did this project happen?

NH: I wrote about Ben in *Songbook*, and he got in touch. (I wrote about the wonderful lyrics to his song "Smoke," and Ben pointed out that they were just about the only ones he hadn't written in his entire recorded output. But he was amused, rather than hurt.) We stayed in touch, I went to see his shows when he was in London, and then he asked if I'd like to have a go at some words for an album he was making with William Shatner (!). How could I resist? I submitted two songs and they used one of them, and the song turned out well. It's called "That's Me Trying," and it's about a very bad dad of Shatner's age. Aimee Mann was brought in to sing background, and Bill did his declaiming thing. It was a lot of fun. And then Ben asked if I'd like to have a go at a whole record.

AK: There is a distinct Hornby-ness in "Picture Window" from that album ("You know what hope is? / Hope is a bastard / Hope is a liar / A cheat and a tease / Hope comes near you? / Kick its backside / Got no place in days like these"). It's equally heart-breaking and humorous in its storytelling, which works so nicely with Folds' style. What were some of the challenges in bringing your narrative style to music?

NH: There were no challenges! The challenges were all Ben's, I think. I just wrote very short short stories with a few rhymes and some choruses, emailed them over, and then Ben went off and wrote tunes for them. He has an astonishing melodic facility, and he writes very quickly. "Your Dogs," which is one of my favourites, took him about three hours. I sent him the lyrics one evening, he sent me a rough version on mp3—it didn't seem very rough at all to me—the following lunchtime. Actually, the challenge was in finding something that caught his attention. Sometimes he'd send me a note saying, politely, "I got nothing," if something I'd sent him hadn't snagged him, so I wrote probably twice as many as we needed. He had to do a lot more work than me, in the recording and arranging and producing, so that seemed absolutely fair enough.

AK: Let's move on to another collaboration—*The Believer*. You've done an enormous amount of writing for the McSweeney's/*Believer* gang. Can you speak to where your column for *The Believer* began in 2003 and how it evolved over the following decade?

NH: I'd known Dave Eggers and his wife Vendela for two or three years before *The Believer* started. I remember going to the McSweeney's offices when I was on book tour, and Vendela showed me the first issue of the magazine, and I thought, oh, wow, I'd love to write something for this. And I kept dropping hints, telling Vendela how beautiful it looked, but she didn't say anything. And then when I got home she asked if I'd like to write a column about music. I'd recently stopped writing for *The New Yorker*, after a brief and unhappy spell as their music critic, and I really didn't want to do that again. But I'd just gone on the Salinger binge described in the very first column, so I suggested that I write something about reading—about what I read and why. Because of the no-snark rules of the magazine, I had to censor myself a couple of times, and my relationship with the editors (who I imagined as puritan yet somehow promiscuous white-robed vegetarian nudists) became a running gag in the column. I really love doing it, even if I have to take time out every now and again. My reading has become more disciplined, and I make wiser choices. The column changed my reading life forever, and for the better.

AK: I'm glad you brought up *Wild*, which was released in the US right at the time of this interview. If I'm not mistaken, this is your second screenplay based on a memoir featuring a woman on a personal journey—whether intentionally or otherwise—of self-discovery (*Wild* chronicling the thousand-mile solo hike of Cheryl Strayed, and *An Education* following a the complex romantic experiences of Lynn Barber). How did you become involved in these projects, and what did the early stages of your adaptation process look like?

NH: My wife is an independent producer—we met because she worked on *Fever Pitch*, the first (English) film based on my book. We'd always wanted to work together again, but I was writing books and she was having kids (mine, I hasten to add). But when I read Lynn Barber's essay in *Granta*, I showed it to her and suggested that it would make a pretty good movie. I hadn't thought of writing it myself, but when she started looking for a writer, I felt very proprietorial. So we took it from there. And six years later—hey presto!—we had a movie. *Wild* was different. I read the book when it came out, loved it, and tracked down the people who owned the rights. That turned out to be Reese and her producing partner Bruna.

The early stages were very different in each case. *An Education* was a slow burn—I probably wrote two books while we were developing it. The original piece was so short that I was groping for shape, and for the flesh that had to go on the bones. We couldn't find the money for it for a long time. We knew we'd had to cast an unknown in the lead, and that's not attractive to funders. *Wild* went like a train. Reese had a small window of availability, and it was thirteen months from my first conversation with her to the last day of shooting. I did two drafts in three months, then worked with Jean-Marc Vallee intensely just before the shoot.

AK: Was there anything particularly interesting about working with someone else's nonfiction, generating a new product out of someone else's life?

NH: For me the interesting thing about adaptation—any adaptation—is the chance it gives me to work with material that I couldn't have generated myself. However different I try to make my books, I'm still stuck with the limits of my own imagination and experience. With *Wild* and *An Education*, I could use my skills as a dramatist and writer of dialogue on stuff that I connected with deeply but that wasn't my stuff.

AK: Several of your books have been brought to the big screen [*Fever Pitch* (x2), *High Fidelity*, *A Long Way Down*, and now *About a Boy* for both a feature film and a new television series]. How involved have you been in the productions?

NH: The first *Fever Pitch* was atypical. Film 4 in England asked me to have a go at adapting, and I was in no position to turn work down—my first novel hadn't been published, my first son had just been born, I didn't know for sure that writing was going to work for me professionally. And I was turning my memoir into something fictional, so the challenge seemed interesting. I haven't really been involved in anything as closely since then—I'd rather get on with the next idea than spend years picking over the bones of the last one, or the one before last. I've trusted the people involved, enjoyed my dealings with them, and have always supported their right to make what they wanted. The *About A Boy* TV series, however, is really nothing to do with me or my work. That's an adaptation of the movie, not of the book, and I didn't even know it was happening until just before it went out. When I sold the movie rights, I sold all rights. That's OK. The money was good!

AK: Your characters are such a dynamic and memorable force in your novels. When you see these characters on the screen, portrayed by guys like Cusack and Grant, do you find yourself learning things about the characters that you maybe hadn't considered before? What was it like the first time an actor just nailed one of your favorite scenes from a book?

NH: I just don't see it that way. The process of adaptation is actually quite radical—my characters are interpreted by a screenwriter, then by a director, then by an actor (and an editor, and a producer, etc., etc., etc.). The characters must of necessity change. I can see how my books are responsible for the movies, but hundreds of tiny creative decisions mean that I end up only vaguely recognizing them. I'm not complaining about this process. It's just what has to happen. All characters are functions of narrative, and if the narrative changes, which it invariably has to, then these people are responding in ways that I hadn't anticipated. I'm always surprised if they keep stuff. There are chunks of *High Fidelity*, for example, especially John's to-camera monologues, that do come from the book, and that feels much weirder than any departure.

AK: You pay great homage to early TV sitcoms in your new novel *Funny Girl*, which follows Sophie Straw, a comedienne seeking stardom in the '60s. What sitcoms did you draw from in developing this character and her experiences in the world of television production?

NH: There was an English strand and an American strand. Ray Galton and Alan Simpson, who wrote *Steptoe and Son* (Americans might remember the remake, *Sanford and Sons*) and several other hit shows, were as sharp, funny and observant as any novelist or playwright working at the time, and they have never got the literary credit they deserve—they have been as big an influence on my work as any novelist. I wanted the writers of my fictional show to be as smart as they were. But nobody in English comedy wrote about women, really, so I had to import American influences to do what I wanted to do with the book.

AK: In an interview with your publisher to promote *Funny Girl*, you spoke about the influence of American television on British programming (you pointed specifically to Lucille Ball and other sitcoms). Do you think that there has also been a shift in the opposite direction, particularly with the American success of shows like *Downton Abbey* and *Sherlock* (I'm also thinking about how sketch comedy in America was forever changed by Monty Python)?

NH: Oh, God, I hope *Downton Abbey* isn't an influence on American TV...I think everyone in the UK is in awe of the American dramas that we've been watching in the last few years—*The Wire*, *Mad Men*, *Breaking Bad*, etc., etc. We don't really have that new cable culture of long-form serious (and expensive) television yet; although there are signs that this is beginning to change. But over the last forty or fifty years, influence has been much more fluid. We read the same books, listen to the same music, watch the same movies and TV shows. The modern world has made all this possible. It could be that nationality has no real part to play in the creation of a distinctive voice any more.

AK: Thank you for speaking with me, Nick. It's been a pleasure. Let's sign off with the traditional question: *So what's next?*

NH: I'm adapting Nina Stibbe's book *Love, Nina* for a five-part BBC series, and I'm writing a movie for Jason Reitman. That's probably the whole of 2015, although I'd like to squeeze an original TV drama in there somewhere, because I have an idea I'm excited about. I have a US book tour to get through first...

Laura Jean Moore
2014 Zora Neale Hurston Fiction Prize Winner

The Crossroads

At the crossroads outside of Centre, the road is paved where it once was hard-packed earth. There is little traffic where it once was constant and the summers have grown long. A billy goat chews the clover by the side of the road. The grass is tall around him and his tufted chin drops into the greenery as he rips up weeds and grinds them between his yellowed molars. A copperhead slithers across the black-sheened asphalt and curls in the warm gravel behind the goat, waiting for the field mice that will scamper from the vegetation after dark. The sun sits high to the west. The goat lifts his head; grass flowers hang out the side of his mouth. His ears twitch. The heat ripples the air.

RJ is tired. He's been walking three days to get to Centre, which is two days longer than he thought he'd need to. They say that Centre is booming, that the retail outlets outside of town are hiring so fast you can't stay poor, and he's in need of a job. His tennis shoes are laced tight, and his soles grip the road like old friends. Ahead he sees a billy goat step into the road. Beyond the goat is the figure of a man who looks to be as black and tall as himself.

They meet like travelers from the same country in a foreign land. Ike Z. extends his hand, RJ shakes it, and they offer their names to each other. They are not in the center of the crossroads, but are near enough that the meeting feels pre-ordained, that it might be that they have been expecting each other. The billy goat ignores them and continues crossing to the other side. The snake sunbathes among the weeds.

—You know where Centre is? asks RJ.

—Just leaving, says Ike Z. There's nothing worth staying for.

—I heard they got so many jobs that they're giving them away. Hardly any experience needed.

—Oh maybe out on the other side of town. Big retailers have opened up and they surely need employees. But downtown? Ain't nothing to do. Looks like a ghost town.

—Well that's about the worst news I've heard since I hit the road. I've been walking so long my soul is tired. I could really do for something to eat, not to mention the work I was hoping for. Everything in Enterprise is pretty much the same. All boarded up and empty. Everyone drives around in their cars instead of walking down the sidewalk. I guess downtown just couldn't compete with the Valu-mart by the highway, and Lord knows I don't wanna work in a place like that again. I had heard Centre was different, is all. I was hoping Centre had something to offer.

—Sure enough it's got as much charm as a cemetery. I was ready for some wilder land. I thought I'd head west and see what I found.

—Well, you must be turned around cause this road runs north to south.

—Not that one.

Ike Z. points at the road crossing their own. The goat has walked cattacorner to where they are standing and the southwestern sun shines on his back like white fire.

RJ looks at the western road and then down the southerly path he has been taking. It disappoints him to learn that Centre is no different than Enterprise. He was hoping for a job in a real thriving community, where the downtown was still the downtown, where everything was as it should be. He scrutinizes Ike Z. The man's hat has clearly been stepped on and never fixed. His beard is new, but scruffy. The knuckles on his hands are calloused, like he has known work, if not recently, then sometime in the past, and his clothes are clean.

—What's west of here? asks RJ.

—Probably more of the same, says Ike Z.

RJ steps back to consider his options again. As he does, he suddenly hears the distinct ch-ch-ch-ch-ch-ch-ch-ch of a snake's rattle. He glances behind him and sees the coil of a copperhead near his ankle.

—Don't think you oughtta go that way anymore, says Ike Z.

RJ tip-toes away from the snake and onto the road, then takes off running, making a sharp right at the crossroads. Ike Z. yells at him to hold on, and fifty yards down the western asphalt, RJ stops and waits for Ike Z. to catch up. They turn and walk together, oblique of Centre, and leave the goat and snake to eat what can be found.

The road west has been paved less recently than the one they left. To the south, oak and pitch and sugar gum trees crowd together, blocking the horizon. To the North, electric wires run between low wooden posts demarcating other men's property. Ike Z. walks at a turtle's pace, as though he is saving for another sprint. RJ cannot keep parallel, and pulls ahead, his feet quickening with the race of his thoughts.

—Car, says Ike Z.

And, as if out of nowhere, a car approaches from behind. It needs a new muffler, and the sound makes RJ wince. He kicks a smashed and bleached out paper cup on the ground.

—I guess there's somewhere to go to if that car's headed our way, says RJ.

—There's always somewhere, says Ike Z.

They plod in line for the better part of the afternoon. As the sun dims, the first hint of a destination appears before them. Street lights. Illuminated by a spotlight is a green metal sign, weather beaten and three feet off the ground: Askew, Alabama; Population 1618.

—Funniest name I ever heard, says RJ.

—Can't say it's much stranger than where you come from.

—Fair enough.

The men keep walking, and beyond the town line, the woods break into large lots with old houses set on brick foundations. Each has its own version of a front porch; some have wrap-arounds and others a side veranda. Two are under renovation, with scaffolding hiding the front entrance. They pass a coral-colored stucco and then a white-sided beauty. They continue toward town. The old money residential area changes into doctor's and law offices set up in converted houses. Beyond these is a gas station and a string of retailers peddling everything from auto parts to children's clothing.

—This place looks live enough, says Ike Z.

—And I smell french fries, says RJ.

He raises his head and inhales the aroma of hot grease. They come to the main crossroad, and across the street is *Don's Restaurant*, a meat and three in a converted school house. Bellies aching, they enter like pilgrims arrived at the temple of their seeking. A short white woman with her hair pulled up in a stringy ponytail greets them.

—Two? she asks.

Ike Z. nods. They pass the kitchen on their way to a red booth and RJ sees the cook, a heavy-set man three shades darker than himself and looking like he could raise the dead. The cook looks at RJ like he knows him, and RJ feels as rattled as the snake's tail he heard behind him that morning.

—How we gonna pay for this? RJ asks after they have their menus.

—I've got it, says Ike Z.

They order pork chops and potatoes with a shared side of green beans. The restaurant is mostly empty, except for a couple whispering to themselves by the left bank of windows and a family of four who are picking at their food like they've never seen vegetables that weren't raw.

—Ain't seen a place like this in probably 40 years, says Ike Z.

—How old are you? asks RJ.

—Old enough to teach you a thing or two, says Ike Z.

The cook surprises them at the side of their table, plates in hand. He leans his sweaty eyes into RJ's periphery, scrutinizing the young man's face like a topographical map.

—What're you staring at? asks RJ, knife and fork in hand.

—Your foolish mug, says the cook. I've been waiting for you to show up some fifteen years. Sure as I'm standing I never thought you'd come in on a Friday night.

Ike Z. starts laughing.

—You can blame that on me, he says.

RJ frowns.

—Look man, I don't know you and I don't know what the hell you're talking about. And as for you, he says, pointing his knifes at Ike Z.'s chest, I sure as hell don't know what you're on about.

Ike Z. grabs the end of RJ's knife as quick as if he was catching a fly.

—You ever point a knife at me again and you'll learn quick.

RJ wants to ask what he'll learn but he feels uneasy. He lowers his silverware and looks up at the cook.

—Well then, when were you expecting me? he asks.

—I sure enough thought your momma would be in with you while you was still young.

—My mother's been dead seven years.

The cook nods his head.

—That explains some things, he says.

—Look Don, whyn't you let us eat? We can talk this over with our bellies full, says Ike Z.

The cook looks down at the two of them, then he walks off like he agrees.

—How'd you know his name? RJ asks.

—It's Don's Restaurant, ain't it?

—But that don't always mean—

—Lucky guess, then.

The men tear into their supper, ripping the meat into tiny bites and scooping the green beans and potatoes into their mouths. They follow the meal with cold sweet tea and RJ believes he's never had food so good. The moment their plates are empty, Don is ready to clear the table. He tells Ike Z. to go out back by the bonfire and they can have some beers.

—We don't even know this man, says RJ.

—He seems to know you, says Ike Z. Don't that make you the least bit curious?

—As curious as I ever am about a crazy man. This just isn't what I had planned.

—I thought you didn't have a plan.

—Well, I did, says RJ, muttering to no one.

Behind the restaurant is a small yard cordoned by chicken wire. In the center is a bonfire of wood scraps with nails still in them. The straight metal glows red in the heat. Though it is early summer, the evening is cool, and RJ is thankful for the burning warmth. He pulls a folding chair from the short concrete porch, and sits close enough that the flames illuminate his face. The cook joins them, bringing three bottles of cold beer. Ike Z. takes his and sits on RJ's left. The cook sits on the right. They face the fire, sipping their beer and wiping the condensation from the glass on their pants. The cook looks away from the flames and stares at RJ again, squinting.

—You sure don't look like her, says Don.

—They say I look like my father, says RJ.

—They say right.

—What is this? Who are you? My people are from Enterprise and as far as I know none of them have ever been to As-skew or even heard of this place.

—You take it easy, says Ike Z.

—My name's Don Glenn and I'm your momma's brother.

—My mother didn't have a brother, says RJ.

—True she didn't have a lot of things but a brother's not one of them.

—I wondered about this, says Ike Z.

—You are the most confounding person I ever met, says RJ.

—I'm just saying I wondered what might happen tonight. Don't ever know what's gonna happen when you let a stranger come along.

RJ ignores him, thinking Ike Z. might be the crazy one.

—If you're her brother, then tell me something only someone who loved her would know.

Don leans back in his chair and chugs the rest of his beer. He stares into the flames like he is conjuring up old memories, bringing back what was. A black, mangy dog scrapes at the outside of the chicken wire like he's expecting scraps, and Ike Z. tells him to scat, then rolls up his sleeves, exposing dark tattoos of writhing snakes on his forearms. RJ stares.

—She would always take the last biscuit without asking, says Don.

—No she wouldn't, says RJ. She'd give it to me.

—Then I'll tell you this: she had a black mole on her left shoulder blade and she could make her elbows crack when she extended them. She was born in Enterprise and gave birth to you in a church, and she wouldn't say who your father was.

—Then how do you know that I look like him?

—Cause you're the spitting image of our preacher.

—My mother said my father was dead before I was born.

—He shot himself five months 'fore you was born. One of the other girls in church didn't feel like keeping his secrets as much as Sarah.

—That was her name, says RJ.

—Well he said he knew her, says Ike Z., getting up to look through the junk pile in the corner of the yard. The mountain of artifacts sits in a jumble of bedsprings and record players and side tables and three legged chairs. Ike Z. finds a scratched up guitar and pulls it from the tangle. He tunes it by the fire while the men continue forming words from the night air.

—How did she die? asks Don.

—Pneumonia, says RJ. One winter she couldn't get warm enough, kept saying she was cold, and then she started coughing. We thought she'd be well as soon as spring came, but she was gone by the New Year.

—Well she told me she was just tired. I guess she's always liked to smooth over the truth.

Don puts his hands forward, warming his palms in front of the flames.

—She talked to you all those years and never said a word about me?

—Not a word, says RJ. He begins pacing away from the fire, looking sideways at this man, his mother's brother. Every time Don makes sense, he goes back and makes crazy. Ike Z. starts a song, a broken piece of metal pipe on his finger, the guitar crying at their silence. Beyond the chicken wire, down the road from whence they came, the storefronts and gas station are dark. None of the homes are illuminated and even the street lights have gone out. The whole town is contained by blackness, with the light of their bonfire isolated like a star in the nighttime.

—This place sure closes up early, says RJ, kicking the junk pile at the edge of the yard. The dog has come back, and he scratches at the chicken wire to get in.

—Can't you get rid of him? asks RJ.

—Hard to get rid of a dead dog, says Don. He gets up and kicks at the fence where the dog persists. The dog jumps toward the sound and then disappears into the darkness.

—I used to have a dog like that, says Ike Z. He begins to hum, a guttural tune that sounds like what the ground would sing if it could speak. RJ frowns again.

Don gets some more wood scraps from the junk pile. He steps on a broken chair and then throws the pieces on the fire. The resin boils out of the wood, crackling and throwing sparks. RJ thrusts his hands in his pockets and rocks on his heels, staring at the red flames. He tries to think about his day, but can't remember what he was doing that morning. He's been on the road so long that all he can remember is the road. It feels like years since he said goodbye to his neighbors in Enterprise, since he left a note on his stepfather's door saying he was leaving for something better.

—I think I might need to find a place to rest, says RJ.

—You two don't have a place to stay? asks Don.

—Right here is good enough for me, says Ike Z.

Don sits in RJ's chair and leans toward Ike Z.'s guitar, squinting at the stranger's face.

—I've seen you before too, says Don. But it's probably been years since you've been in town.

—It's true I even forgot about Askew, says Ike Z. Didn't even recognize the road I was taking when I walked it with this fellow. It's sure been a long time.

RJ hears a crack, louder than the pops of the wood in the wire.

—Y'all hear that? he asks.

The men look to the east. Twigs break under foot, but whose, they cannot see. Out of the black, a woman, dressed in a church dress, approaches the chicken wire. The fire lights up the deep brown of her face, and she grips the wire with gloved hands. RJ can't believe his eyes.

—Give me back my boy, says the woman.

Ike Z. stops playing and pivots on his seat.

—He's just come to visit, says Don, unbothered by the apparition. Come later than I expected. Always thought you'd come first and bring him with you, but we both know you held out for a more natural way.

RJ walks slowly to the wire, staring at the woman's face. Standing across from him is his mother, as real as morning light. He reaches his hand and touches the parts of her fingers sticking through the wire. She smiles at him.

—Come with me, baby. I've come to get you, she says.

RJ turns and faces the other men.

—What is this place? I just touched my mother's hands, as warm as the day she died.

—We know, says Don.

—Don't listen to them, says the woman. Walk out of there and come with me, baby.

Ike Z. begins to play again, humming over a picked melody.

—What'd you do on Tuesday? he sings, quietly. What'd you do before you left town?

—I've been on the road so long, I don't hardly remember, says RJ.

—Oh you remember, says Ike Z. It's not so long you don't know.

RJ stares at this woman, his mother, and then squats on the ground, covering his head with his hands.

—I was just trying to get to Centre, he says. I heard they have something for me to do.

—They do, baby, says the woman. I come from Centre just as sure as you sit there. Come with me and leave these men to themselves.

RJ stays where he sits, staring at the soft earth beneath his feet. The shadows change with the flickering of the bonfire.

—What'd you do on Tuesday, Ike Z. sings. What'd you do before you left town?

—He shot himself, as true as me, says Don, and heads into the restaurant to get more beer. RJ bolts upright and sees tears on his mother's face.

—You don't have to stay here, she says, her fingertips wiggling in the wire. They told me it was an accident, and you don't have to stay.

Ike Z. drops his head, shaking and bouncing his knee to the tune he plays at the night. RJ grabs the chicken wire for support with one hand, and bends over, close to puking. He closes his eyes and tries to remember. There is the note on his stepfather's house. He is home again, making lunch, and he remembers to get a jacket before he leaves. Even in summer a jacket might be necessary. It is the kind of thing that a person can't leave behind. He opens the door to the closet, and there is his shotgun, propped on some boxes, leaning on the coats. He reaches for the jacket and the shotgun falls.

—It was the note that confused them, says the woman. They thought you meant to go. But I know my baby. He was just looking for work, she says. He was just heading out for a new life instead of the old.

RJ touches his chest, and then feels up the side of his neck where a wound should have been. He is whole. There is no bloody flesh. He leans his head on the chicken wire, and his mother shifts so that her forehead is on his own, pressing through the barrier.

—Come with me, she says. Her breath smells like honeysuckle.

Don returns with more beer. He hands a glass to Ike Z., who sets down the guitar and drinks the cold brew like water.

—Easy mistake, says Ike Z. after a long swig. He begins to laugh. Don laughs with him, and their voices echo, unceasing. The warmth from the bonfire suddenly feels too hot, and RJ sweats through his clothes. He lunges for the guitar and swings it at Ike Z.'s head, but Ike Z. stops him with one block of the arm, yanking the instrument from RJ's hands.

—You still have a lot to learn, he says.

RJ backs away. He looks at Don, who seems suddenly old, as though he has been cooking for too long, drinking for too long, sitting in this yard for much too long. Panicked, RJ runs out of the yard, through the restaurant and out the front door. His mother is there, and she takes his hand like she used to when he was a boy, leading him down the road.

—I knew you didn't mean to, she says, shaking her head. She pulls him ahead and RJ stumbles along, turning back to see the bonfire, raging toward the sky. The dark figures of Ike Z. and Don move around yellow and red flames, blending into the shadows and then becoming distinct again. The hollow guitar sings like a choir of demons.

Mother and son walk east, past the darkened doorways of the businesses and stores of Askew. As they make their way, several cars pass them, speeding on the open road. Wind rustles the forest, and gradually, RJ begins to feel safe again.

—There's work in Centre? he asks, slipping his hand from his mother's grip.

—Plenty to do downtown, she says. And the streets are full of people you'll recognize. I'm afraid you'll never get to meet your father. That dog was late again tonight, and I got you first.

RJ nods his head. In his memory, he can almost see a third figure in the shadows, dancing around the flames.

At the crossroads, they turn south. The goat is gone, and the snake is dead, flattened by a car in the middle of the road. Sarah slips her arm into the crook of RJ's elbow. They walk like this, even as the sun rises, until they are home.

Liza Porter
2014 Gabriela Mistral Poetry Prize Finalist

Blue Gloves, Stars

Forgive me, I have almost forgotten your face
in the ten years you've been gone, I have ruined
your blue cashmere gloves, there is pencil lead smudged
on the fingers of the right one from writing
outside in winter, a gaping hole
on the tip of the middle finger, a snag on the knuckle of the thumb
where the yarn is unraveling like time, forgive me
I spilled coffee on one of your stories—the long one about green glass
and stars, a woman abandoned in the dark
I have changed the glass and stars to the pale sea blue
of your gloves, but most of all forgive me
for pretending the story is mine, I know that is cheating
you, me, the dead, the living, but think of the universe
its fickle lights and lies—I want something
of you to be me, I want you to be a story, or a film I can watch every day
I'll keep watching and watching until the stars say
their last lines and fall dead on the floor, the celluloid flops
on its reel after the credits roll, the sound of a train going by but not
the ending of the movie will comfort me, as if seeing
death on the screen can cancel dying itself or at least conceal you
as you fly across a sweeping panorama of the Pacific Ocean
where we floated as children and built sand castles as high
as our unlived lives, I forgive you for being the first to die—
before her time people say when someone leaps
and rises above the earth to reach the other world
before we think they should, forgive me
if I am not convinced this is true.

Michael Salcman

That Summer Conference

for Deborah Digges (1950-2009)

At the end of the week, I'd written ten—
a poem in two voices, a poem about objects seen far away
and up close in magnification: useful exercises
I've never been able to do again.
You said read them to me, making a few quick edits
and lightning fast struck a comma here, a word there.

You said read them again,
the bud of your face closing, shuttering its stare.
You listened hard, I could tell,
mouth moving in and out, squeezing each iamb—
above your upper lip a single drop of quivering moisture
and a ten-mile pile of red hair, already graying.

It took thirty minutes for you to come out of your spell.
You said we were done. I was dismissed at once
as if only another disciple blessed by your touch,
by the hand that ordinarily swept away
the sparrows you heard speaking in tongues,
their shadows banging in the one treeless plaza on campus.

I didn't argue. Gentle kindness was your strength
and having your ear that day as good as sex.
But saying good-bye felt more like a death in childhood.
We were done in different ways, you sooner than most,
like a bee that had stung in Plath and fallen off. I said thanks
and moved on, my palms growing as red as strawberry jam.

Cara Cotter

The Movie Men

"Either I'm dead right or I'm crazy."—*Mr. Smith Goes to Washington*

I met the "uncles" for the first time at my dad's wake, when I was fourteen. None of the uncles were actually related to Dad or me. They were the seven other guys who'd lived in the baseball house with him during his years at Colgate. I'd heard their voices on our answering machine, and I'd idly checked out their kids on the Christmas cards—if their daughters were better-looking than me, if they had boys my age.

But it was the movies I recognized them from when the first few walked in, somber-faced, wearing long coats over their suits. Not home movies, since Dad's college days were years before he got his hands on a video camera, but the movies Dad would find on TV, late at night.

"Vi, Vi," he'd say to Mom, who'd be falling asleep on the couch. "Doesn't Bogie in this one remind you of Sweeney?" Or, when we came across *Field of Dreams* for the third time in one weekend, he'd sit up, laughing, going, "Finally clicked—Costner's a dead ringer for Martin."

Dad and Mom met in college, so she always knew who he was talking about, even when Mary and I were a little lost. And she'd always say, "I don't really see it, Jimbo."

"C'mon," he'd say, running his hand up and down just in front of his face as if demonstrating something: "It's the hangdog eyes," or "It's that Midwest cornbread vibe," right over Mom's protestation that Costner wasn't actually Midwestern, or "But you got to admit, they're both so starkly *German*."

Mom was appalled by the last one. "You wouldn't dare say so to Bosch."

Dad didn't like that, so he called up his buddy Bosch in D.C. Mary and I ran upstairs to listen on the upstairs extension as Dad let it drop that we'd been watching *Indiana Jones and the Last Crusade* and dammit if the one Nazi captain didn't look like he could be Bosch's brother.

There was a moment of silence and a click. Mary and I thought Dad's friend had hung up before the voice came back with a roar of laughter, saying he'd dropped the fucking phone and letting loose a slew of R-rated words that I hadn't known could be said so affectionately.

Sometimes Mom would humor Dad by agreeing, which seemed to frustrate him more than her disagreeing because he could tell she didn't really see it. "Don't *patronize* me, Vi," he'd say, raggedly. I only ever heard them argue with real heat over stupid little things, but that line could set them off. For all Dad's comfortable jokes about Mom being the breadwinner, for all that he loved having time for volunteer coaching, losing his bank job left a dent in his soul.

I didn't get that then, but Mom did, and right around when I'd start panicking about how many of my classmates' parents had divorced, her voice would soften, and she'd admit that no, she couldn't see it at all. Dad would groan about how she had no imagination, but that would be the end of it. Mary and I didn't give his comparisons much heed. He'd call us his Katherine Hepburn (not the Hepburn who Mary hoped to look like) and Maureen O'Hara. Especially since I wasn't a redhead like Maureen, I didn't get it. "Look at Maureen in a black-and-white and tell me you don't see yourself," Dad insisted. Her face was slightly squared-off like mine, but my bone structure added up to *striking* in place of even *pretty*, while the iconic actress defined *striking beauty*. We figured Dad was being generous and, like most dads, a little kooky.

But when Dad died and the uncles showed up, I saw he'd been right all along. They introduced themselves as Uncles Tobias, Pete, Mark, so on, not the last names Dad usually tossed around, making for too many new names to match to too many tall men, particularly then. But I could pin the man with the mournful dark eyes that seemed to take over his face as Uncle Bogie, and the tallest man, with thinning hair, I recognized as Uncle Costner, though the resemblance to the actor was really just in the crinkling of his eyes and maybe the voice. The gaunt, straight-backed man with the hawk nose, I felt terrible for thinking of as Uncle Nazi, especially when he was the first one to grab me up in a hug and the first one to make me smile, when he said with a straight face, "I was with your dad every day for four years of college, and I was with your dad all four times he got arrested." (At the time I was sure he was joking.)

I didn't slip out loud, though, until night, when Mom insisted the uncles come back to the house. Surely we were too tired, they protested, but Mom wanted her girls to get to visit with them. I'd already been following them around at the wake, hanging onto their every word of Dad, leaving Mary to be older and responsible and stay with Mom by the coffin.

We had so much food and drink from neighbors and relatives I imagined it amounted to more than Dad had consumed in his whole life. While Mary grabbed beers and Mom put out sandwiches, the uncle who'd come all the way from Georgia asked me, "Do you have any coffee, sweetheart?"

I hadn't ever heard a Southern accent like his in real life before, and with his curly, prematurely gray hair and startlingly bright eyes, I thought him exceptionally handsome for an old guy. Our coffee machine was buried somewhere under the fruit baskets, I explained, and pointed to a packaged bag of gourmet teas and the like. "Sorry, Uncle Ashley, hot cocoa?"

He paused. "Pardon, Laurey hun, what's that again?"

Turning red, I repeated the part about cocoa, but he'd actually heard the "Uncle Ashley" bit all right the first time and wanted to know if that's what my daddy said to call him.

I had to tell him not exactly and explain about having seen part of *Gone With the Wind* with Dad one night.

"At least I'm not Uncle Scarlett," he said, smiling, and agreed to the cocoa. When I came back with it, the other uncles wanted to know if I had names for them, and Uncle Nazi said, oh brother, he hoped he wasn't Uncle Nazi or something.

"You got types?" —*The Thin Man*

I didn't mean to start hanging out at the tattoo parlor. I found tattoos on guys to be a turn-off, I'd never managed to last five minutes with a temporary tattoo or henna before wanting to scrub it off, and Mom would probably cry if I ever got one. But after turning eighteen I found myself lingering around the parlor down the street from my high school. And one day I walked through the door, nodded at the guy with eyebrow piercings manning the counter, and circled the shop, looking at the photographs of tattoos pinned to the wall, especially the quotes.

"Just browsing," I said, if anyone asked.

The only one who acknowledged me at all was the guy with piercings, one of the artists. He was usually just behind the counter when I came in, but I'd spotted him etching a blue bird on a girl's shoulder one day. His only visible tattoos ran up his left arm, and I assumed he'd done them himself. Scales started on his middle finger and spread up to spiral around his wrist, becoming the tail of a dragon that took up his entire arm. It was stylized like the sea monster on an old map, and old-style font letters marked up his shoulder. I thought they read "Here Be," but I'd never gotten close enough to tell for sure.

"I'm beginning to think you just like me," he said the sixth time I came in, crossing the dragon arm over the other.

I jumped. That thought hadn't occurred to me, since I'd grouped him with his tattoos—fascinating but not at all part of my world. I supposed he was twenty-something, okay verging on attractive if he took the piercings out. "I like your work," I said.

"Just trying to get up the nerve?" he said, looking me over. I thought he might be arching a brow, but it was hard to tell under all that metal. "Let me guess: you want a classy little line. Maybe in Latin."

"I don't know Latin."

"Neither do I, really, so there's some risk there. But it's usually the stock phrases. *Amor vincit omnia, bibo ergo sum, cave canem—*"

SAT root words and little bits from history class filled in more than I'd expected. "*Bibo ergo*—I drink, therefore I am?"

"Fairly fucking popular," piercings guy said, nodding.

"That's pretty lame," I said, "for something meant for forever." I thought about my grandfather when he went swimming, the way the skin sagged like drapery over his rib cage, and imagined stretched-out letters and fading colors on such a shifted canvas.

"This boy last week," he said conversationally, "wanted 'Thank You' right here." He planted a hand over the belt loops of his jeans. "In case he forgot to say it."

"Now that's *gross*."

He tilted his head. "How old are you? Is that what you're doing, plotting out what you'll get when you're of age?"

"No, actually I'm—" I hesitated. "Well, I don't know what words I'd want."

It was Dad's words I wanted to keep forever. The end of high school neared, and fourteen suddenly seemed a long time ago. That scared me. Dad didn't seem like a long time ago. He never could be, for me, and sewing his voice into my skin would make sure it stayed that way.

But I couldn't boil him down to one motto, and his words were always borrowed. When I was little and he'd drawl, "It's not the years, honey, it's the mileage," or joke he'd lasso the moon for his girls, I thought he was coming up with that stuff himself. When we'd finally gotten around to clearing out some of dad's clothes and papers almost two years after, I'd trembled at finding a leather-bound journal, counting on its pages to add to my hoard of Dad's words. But it was mostly blank. The first fifteen pages were filled, but with one-liners, mostly from John Wayne and Jimmy Stewart movies. There were no dates, though Mom thought the first faded pencil marks might go as far back as Dad's high-school movie usher job, and the last, in still-bright pen, were from *A Knight's Tale—my* movie. Dad took me and my friend to it in seventh grade because we couldn't get into PG-13s ourselves. He'd grumbled but then laughed so resoundingly in the dark that I'd been mortified, more so when he tried to discuss the movie's high points on the drive home, while I just wanted to gossip about how cute Heath Ledger was. Later, though, it became one he and I could agree on renting.

Piercings guy snapped his fingers in front of my face. "You still in there?"

Dad hated being snapped at by anyone. It was treating a man like a dog, he'd say. "I'm thinking," I said. "'Change your stars,' I like that."

"It's pretty," he agreed dubiously. I wanted to be annoyed, but out loud, out of context, the quote sounded stock, vague. To me, it was a reminder how much Dad took from even a fun adventure movie. Dad wrote two lines from *Knight's Tale* in his journal; first "You have been weighed, you have been measured, and you have been found wanting," carefully penned and just as carefully crossed out. "Change your stars," rewriting the sky to lead a better life, was its reply.

But aside from his could've-been-a-contender work frustrations, I didn't want a better life than Dad's. Just one a lot like it. "It's one idea," I said to piercings guy.

He asked for some of the others, but I demurred, saying I had to go.

He pulled out a card, scribbled his cell number on it, and said, "If you decide. Or if you have that birthday."

I'd never had the chance to bring a guy home to Dad. My sister Mary had a succession, dismissively dubbed by Dad as Spicoli, Bill/Ted, and Harvey, as in the silent, invisible seven-foot rabbit. Dad hated nothing more than blank stares. He expected conversation to be a game of catch, a smooth arc of back-and-forth, with both players competent at fielding any topic that might be thrown at them. I wondered how piercings guy would fare in Dad's book, cover aside.

I did take his card. "Do you like baseball?" I asked.

Piercings guy laughed. "Not much for that country club shit, no."

"Ah," I said, "no. Country club stuff would be golf. Same principles to the swing really, but the ball doesn't move."

"I know what golf is," he said, still amused. "Like you said—same shit."

I glanced away from his eyes, to the dragon climbing his arm.

"So, what, that your kinda deal breaker? You only go with guys who bat two hundred?"

"Two hundred's a pretty low bar," I said.

"Hey, all the better. Trust me, high bars never stay high long, if you ever want to get any-fucking-where." This time he caught my flinch at his *fuck*. He clicked his tongue, the metal in it clanging on his teeth. "Shit, you even seventeen?"

"It's not about the years," I said, "I'm just taking my time with the mileage." I waited to see if he'd catch the reference, if he'd play on a quote in reply.

His wink moved his whole eyebrow bar. "Well. Let me know when you're set to rack some up."

I didn't. I stuck his card in my souvenir box and stopped drifting into the shop. I felt like I was supposed to be in my rebel stage, like Mary was when she was eighteen and Dad was alive, but no real McMurphy or Cool Hand Luke was surfacing to shake up my schedule, and there was nothing I really wanted to break away from.

I window-shopped at other places for a while. But I never did get a tattoo. Dad's voice in my head pulled me up short, maybe something I once heard him say, maybe about something else, or maybe only my best guess of what his take would be: *You like it so much, why don't you just put it on a T-shirt?*

"Not just one wish, a whole hatful." —*It's a Wonderful Life*

I kept tabs on the Christmas card boys, to the extent of secret Internet stalking. It started with the College World Series when, all excitement, Mom shouted for Mary and me to rush downstairs, the ballgame turned up to surround sound. We found Mom, phone against her ear, jabbing her finger urgently at the screen. Even count, and the batter swung at a fastball, a little high and outside. Uncle Costner's son was pitching.

"Oh," I said, and "oh," again, as he wound up, knee lifted in perfect form, and fired one straight across the plate. His uniform shirt was light blue, and even from the long camera shot, I could tell his eyes were, too.

Mary stayed and watched for a few minutes. I sat down with my mom and watched Uncle Costner's son's team win the game. Then I went and pulled out Mom's Christmas card file.

There were newspaper clippings from Uncle Costner in there, about his son's high school championship and summer leagues, though he'd sent far fewer since Dad had been gone. The crisp, bright Christmas pictures of the family by the mantle gave me a much better look at the pitcher's face and smile than the quick TV shots and his cap brim had allowed me.

I stole my sister's laptop, logged onto my just-started Facebook account, and found his name right away. And I started plowing through the rest of the uncles' cards, too, with purpose.

I didn't even hear Mary coming in to take her laptop back.

"This seems vaguely Oedipal," Mary said, checking out the pictures over my shoulder. "Obsessing over Dad's friends' kids? Really?"

"I'm not obsessing," I said. "They just seem like the same type I'd like if we just— met."

"You'll meet plenty of guys at college."

"I don't know, I saw the guys you met at college."

Mary made a face at me, lifting an old picture of the Bogie boys in Halloween costumes. "Who's Robin Hood?"

"Actually, he only lives about two hours away—"

Mary took a second look at the picture. "Oh, God, the one dad tried to convince to drive up to take me to *prom*? He was always doing that, especially when the uncles got together to go see a game—this one's boys have a band, and this one's a gentleman, and why can't I bring home a boy capable of saying 'Hi, Mr. Weaver' with a handshake, not a silent nod—"

"I remember," I said, too shortly, and was immediately mad at myself. Mary rarely wanted to talk about Dad. "I mean—"

Mary put down the picture. "Forget it," she said. "And forget this. You're never going to meet these guys. Anyway, isn't the lesson of all that Hollywood stuff you love usually to look for the person who's been there all along, give the schlubby guy a chance?"

"Not my kind of movies," I said. "And it's not like I'm asking for the moon." I didn't expect any guy of my generation ever to tell me I looked like Maureen O'Hara, particularly if I wanted one who'd also want to hit the batting cages with me. "I don't see the problem with doing a lot of looking. Mom swears when she was our age there were plenty of guys who really were gentlemanly and able to banter about anything and still athletic too. They must still exist. Somewhere. Possibly hiding. Or just taking a little more time to grow up."

"Or they don't come that way anymore," Mary said.

"But then there's the boys," I said, waving my hand over the Christmas cards. "They're—like some kind of proof."

"Legends never die." —*The Sandlot*

Dad was five years gone when Uncle Bogie's death showed up on Facebook, by way of both of his sons switching their profile pictures to one of their father when he was young, whip-fit, wearing a squinty smile. Since I'd Facebook-friended the sons, I'd seen updates on how their dad was doing, requests for thoughts and prayers, even one picture where Uncle Bogie's bones all but leapt from his skin. I figured it out before Mom got the phone call from Uncle Ashley.

It was a summer wake, so I was home from college. Dad would've gone, wherever in the world he was, and Uncle Bogie had lived just outside of Buffalo, not a bad drive. But Mom couldn't get out of a business trip, and when I asked Mary to come with me, she said it was weird without Mom, we barely knew him. That wasn't how I felt.

I felt a connection to the Bogie boys beyond the loose, long-distance awareness of each other. There was proof we'd met. There are baby pictures of me and the older boy, propped on a couch like dolls, and Mary and me with both Bogie boys at Niagara Falls, wet and in ponchos for the Cave of the Winds tour. I was six, and yet when I try to recall the sound of the water, all I come up with is movie waterfalls; I try to see myself there, and it's a patchwork jumble made of photographs. I had fourteen years with Dad. I remember about half of them well.

I went thinking I was really prepared. I'd been to wakes since Dad's. My insides froze up every time, but I could deal with scrambling and shock. I could muster small talk of the right weight, a smile that was somber without being one of the pitying ones I hated.

But I walked into an atmosphere of exhale, no coffin, walls of picture-covered poster boards with the quote "I consider myself the luckiest man on the face of the earth," in big, block letters at the top, and over the thrum of a packed parlor, "Centerfield" playing in the background: "A' roundin' third, and headed for home, it's a brown-eyed handsome man…"

I doubled back, struck by tears. I ducked my head down, trying to hide my face in my hair, groping for the ladies' room. From movies I felt acutely aware that if I was noticed like this—a twenty-year-old girl generally unknown to family and friends bursting into instant tears at the wake of a middle-aged man—it looked bad.

Once I made it into a stall, I tried to choke my tears down, feeling I had no right. I kept thinking how my dad had loved the old Lou Gehrig movie with the "luckiest man" quote though he didn't even *like* the Yankees, how this other man who knew and understood and *remembered* Dad was also gone too soon, taking with him all the scraps of conversation and adventure between only them, never again to be recounted in an email to Mom or ever known to me.

Eventually I managed to clean my face of its blotchiness and smeared mascara, but I'd given myself the hiccups and couldn't get rid of them.

I looked for a path to the exit as soon as I stepped out of the ladies', only to find myself facing Uncle Luca Brasi.

"Fellas, fellas, look what I found," he said over his shoulder, even while holding out thick arms to me. "Laurey, I hope you don't mind giving out hugs to a bunch of old gaffers…"

I didn't. I almost started crying again because they weren't that old, not at all, but instead I laughed, still hiccupping, as they took me over to the poster board wall to point out pictures of all of them with long hair and stupid beards, as Uncle Nazi told how Dad got himself and Bogie arrested at a college bar by calling two cops Starsky and Hutch.

The older Bogie boy was making his way down the line of people waiting, shaking hands. He was the one Mary's age, the one I knew from Facebook pictures, which I looked at a little too often, to be handsome in a tall, bony way. When he passed by the uncles, Uncle Luca spun me toward him. "This is Jim's girl," Uncle Luca announced me.

"One of," I corrected and started my condolences spiel, but the older Bogie boy, tired-eyed but very calm, even smiling at me, was already saying, "I know you, you're Laurey," and shaking my hand in a fierce grip. "My dad loved your dad. Talked about him a lot lately."

He staggered me. I finally managed to say, “My dad loved yours too,” and only then did he let go of my hand. Some older woman nearby was calling to him, and suddenly he was saying, “I'm so sorry,” which I was supposed to be saying to him and, to Uncle Luca, “Make sure to show her!” The next thing I knew he was hustling off to more handshakes.

“Show me what?” I asked Uncle Luca immediately.

“The other room,” he answered, adding, dramatically, “more pictures.”

“C'mon, Laurey girl, you'll see,” Uncle Ashley said, stepping up and even offering me his arm. “You know how your Uncle Bogie was a movie star for a minute?”

The Natural, with Robert Redford, filmed in and around Buffalo in summer 1982. Every one of the dozen times I'd seen the movie with Dad, he brought up that somewhere deep in the crowd of “Wrigley Field,” his buddy Bogie was there as an extra. I knew all right.

There wasn't much to the other room but extra elbow space, some more poster boards, a table with burnished medals and trophies, until I saw them.

Photographs of seated men were propped up against the far wall. They looked like cardboard cutouts, old ones, seeped of color so I could barely tell it had ever been there, parchment yellow around the edges. The men, all unknown faces to me, were scaled just shy of life-size and came only waist-high, cut off at the bottom so it looked like their knees grew out of the parlor floor. Lined up side-by-side, they had the look of a bullpen, even though they wore suits, bow ties, hats, nice dress for the 1930s, instead of uniforms.

“Meet some other minor movie stars,” Uncle Ashley told me. “I think you're familiar with their work filling out stadium seating.”

A tanned boy, double-fisting water bottles in dripping hands, elbowed his way to stand next to me and Uncle Ashley. “At last, the girl who called my dad ‘Uncle Bogie?’” he asked me, hoarse-voiced. No question he was the second son, not as recognizable without the ear-to-ear grin of the Christmas cards and much older-looking than he'd been on last year's. “He got such a complex about that.”

“I'm sorry,” I said, while he drained a water bottle. His eyes were wet, too.

“No, a good complex. Like, he went and bought fedoras when he started chemo. Sam Spade, *Casablanca*, that was cool stuff.”

“I think so, too.”

He pressed closer to Uncle Ashley, making us more of a circle among the crowd, then, with a gesture of the water bottle, directed our attention to one of the photograph men. “Remind you of anyone?” he asked me.

“Sure does,” Uncle Ashley said.

Not getting it, I stepped closer, bending for a better look.

This cut-out was a young man in a flat cap, which shadowed half his boyish face. He looked all the skinnier for being scaled down, smaller-than-life; my head could halo his. He sat legs apart and arms folded, assessing, lips parted. A small hole, where the photograph had peeled away to show the paper behind, formed right in the middle of his lips. I brought my finger to it.

"A cigarette used to stick out there," the younger Bogie boy said. "But my dad pulled it off when we were kids. Said the shows were giving us enough ideas." He nodded at me. "You can pick it up."

I did and was surprised by the heft. I knocked on the back and found it was real wood, thin as it was, dark and strong, with none of the give of plywood.

"You see it?" the Bogie boy asked impatiently.

I took another look at the cutout's face. "Jimmy Stewart?"

"Jimmy Stewart?" he said, disappointed, while Uncle Ashley laughed.

"Circa *Mr. Smith*," I added, a little defensive.

"He did have that look, some," Uncle Ashley said. "Skinny guy, dark flop of hair…"

I looked again, this time with expectation. And this time I did see it, not Dad as I'd ever known him, with a broader build and fuller cheeks, but another Jimmy, the baseball boy of his old pictures. It wasn't exact, something profoundly different about the proportion between chin and forehead, but the nose was alike, the assured expression, and the eyes, in distance apart, in intensity, in the worlds that seemed just-barely walled-off behind them, those were really close. So close I didn't know how I hadn't seen it right away, how I could ever not see it again.

"My dad got a hold of this guy for the resemblance," the Bogie boy said, watching my face. "And the rest then just 'cause. Always meant to send this one to your dad as a joke, but he kept him. You see it now?"

"I see it," I said. My stomach had the warm, funny feeling I get right after finishing a coffee. These Bogie boys, who I didn't really know, they knew my dad, grasped a sense of him, *remembered* him without having really known him themselves, as I did theirs, melancholy minor movie star who got Dad into as much trouble as Dad did him.

I think I'll love them a little forever for that, and for insisting that I take the cutout, which sat in the passenger seat while I sang "Centerfield" my whole drive home.

"No man is a failure." —*It's a Wonderful Life*

We wondered, later, if Dad's mix-ups his last summer were actually signs we missed.

"Pleasure to meet you, Mrs. McFly," he said, when putting out his hand to Mary's boyfriend's mother. She'd come to our house to take prom pictures and politely corrected him that it was Mc*Cabe*. Dad, for once, was more mortified than Mary.

A few weeks later, he walked in from a golf day looking perturbed. Dad had *Wonderboy* stitched on his golf bag, like the baseball bat in The Natural, as a self-reminder that the essence of the swing stayed the same. He meant it to be funny but said sometimes people took it for conceit. "Well, I gaffed," he said as he set down his golf bag. "Remember John Murray, Vi?"

Mom didn't. Apparently he was a friend of a friend who Dad had known for some years.

"I spent the whole day calling him 'Bill.'" Dad shook his head even as he grinned, as if he couldn't decide whether he was amused or troubled. For some reason, which he attributed to just seeing *Caddyshack*, he'd honestly thought that was the man's name. Everyone thought he was joking so nobody told him otherwise until John got fed up and told Dad off. Dad made self-deprecating jokes about that mistake all summer. Even I could see it really bothered him.

Dad was grouchy the day we moved Mary into the dorms. I was, too, since Mary's first year of college was my first year of high school, but she got all the attention. School was near enough that she could have commuted, but she wanted the dorms for one reason: college boys.

"Jesus, what is this, a national decline?" Dad said, aghast at the boys spotted on our dorm safari. Some boys had attached a Playstation to the common room TV and barely glanced over at Mary and me hauling boxes before turning back to their game. "These guys make McFly look like Tarzan. Our day, we'd have jumped to help a pretty girl move in."

Mom told him he was being ridiculous and just managed to forestall a technology's-the-death-of-social-skills rant.

He wasn't any happier with the roughhousing guys in jerseys who grabbed the elevator we'd been waiting for. "Hey, fellas, fellas," he started to say, but the door closed.

"Ever heard of respect?" he yelled at the departing elevator. "Don't college coaches teach discipline anymore?"

"Oh my God, he's like a cartoon character," Mary said to me. "Next he'll be shaking his fist."

And I giggled.

"We'll get the next one," Mom told Dad.

Deflated, he hoisted Mary's TV and said, "Forget it. I'll take the stairs again."

We'd finished making Mary's bed and were beginning to wonder what was taking him so long, whether he'd taken a wind break on the sixth floor or something, when someone shouted for help from down the hall.

It was a stroke, the doctors told us later, or rather, told Mom, who told us. Mary, over and over again, somewhere between a chant and shriek, kept going, "I need to see him, I need to see him." I understood her then maybe more than ever. Movies told me nobody was dead for sure till you saw the body and that strokes were a thing people survived, at least the first one.

Maybe that wouldn't have been a blessing. All his life, Dad was an athlete, and with his personality and battered pride, if the stroke had taken his facilities instead of his life, maybe that would have been harder, for him, than winking right out of the world.

But I think sometimes, if that was the deal, I'd take it. Because what I want, even more than a game of catch or that last meaningful conversation, is his company for a few movies more.

"If you build it..." —*Field of Dreams*

I dragged Mary to the batting cages last week. "You're a dope," she said. "This is ridiculous," she said. But she came.

"No jewelry," the guy at helmet rental advised us, and we took off our dangling earrings and Mary her ring, to put in the plastic bag he gave us.

Dad used to take us to the cages. Mary had outgrown it before he died, but I never stopped going. I only quit Little League when Mom finally convinced Dad that overhand-pitch was just too much, and I never took to underhand-pitch softball. Dad kept coaching town baseball even after I wasn't one of his players, and I'd sit at the games with scorebook and little snub pencil, marking up the miniature diamond grids. I got a little rusty myself, but after Dad died, swinging at something coming at me fast seemed like a good idea.

I tapped the plate free of dust and then pulled the bat up and back till my left shoulder was under my chin, my right elbow a firm upright triangle. I pivoted as the first ball came at me, left heel dropping down, right heel rising. Close the door, squish the bug, Dad would say. Maybe I should put that one on a T-shirt.

My balls arced high and far into the mesh, but Mary's rattled against the cage behind her.

"You want me to show you?" I asked, but she waved me off.

"I can remember," she said, red-faced and huffing as she adjusted and took another swing, her arms jolting when she connected.

We used up our ball tokens and packed the gear.

"Laurey?" a voice said. I didn't know the face when I turned, but I liked it.

"I'm Nate Lain," he said. "Your dad coached me?"

It took me a minute. My dad had a lot of baseball boys. "Sure I remember," I said, laughing, "Nate the Great." Really, Dad had him down as *Brando* in his scorebook, his own rebel without a cause. No mouthing off in baseball, Dad would shout at him.

Brando held up his bat in one hand, as if it was a palette, then put his hand in the batting glove over the handle. "I still grip Coach Jim's way," he said, settling both hands on the bat.

Mary fussed with the little plastic bag. I smiled. "Me too," I said. "Thanks for telling me. Means a lot to know somebody else does, too."

Mary clicked her tongue, probably thinking he was a bit young or that I was playing again to Dad's type. But I measure any man off him and his movies because it's my measure for myself. I can't respect a guy with a lousy swing when I spend so much time practicing my own.

"One of you girls getting married?" Brando asked, noticing the diamond ring flashing in the plastic bag.

"Mary's marrying Rambo," I replied.

Mary sighed long-sufferingly, but she seemed, at least, less stressed than when I'd picked her up to hit a few. "He was in Special Forces," she said, "and Laurey, like my father, thinks she's a riot. For God's sake, it's not like my guy has a penchant for headbands or anything."

Rambo was actually crew-cut, round-faced and smiley. He was okay. He didn't have a whole lot to say, but he brought Mom flowers, and if he didn't like my name for him, that didn't stop him from grinning at it.

The uncles should be coming in from all over for Mary's wedding. I'd lightly suggested Mary invite their whole families, but she shut that down fast. She admitted, though, each uncle got a plus one. Whoever they might happen to bring along was entirely on them.

"I think Rambo actually wore a bandana," Brando said. He grinned at me. "I like your T-shirt."

I was wearing one of my *Princess Bride* quote T-shirts. I'd started buying shirts like it all the time, at malls, online, custom made at print shops. They're cheaper than tattoos. Easier to try on and take off. Some subtler than others. This one read, *Fencing, fighting, torture, revenge, giants, monsters, chases, escapes, true love, miracles.* "Thanks," I said easily, "you know, not everyone thinks it means what I think it means."

I could practically hear Mary rolling her eyes behind me.

"Means the movie's got sports in it," he said, still grinning. "But if you were thinking of something else—as you wish."

It was Dad's kind of answer. My kind of answer. A sure sign he could play conversational catch. My grin back actually strained my cheeks. "About that left-handed grip of yours," I said. "Fairly nice-looking. So, can you hit anything these days?"

“Sometimes,” he said, and he took some jingling tokens from his pocket. “If you’re sticking around a minute, you can see for yourself.

“Oh, swing away, Nate,” I said. “We’ll stick around.”

The second he stepped into the cage, Mary grabbed my arm and tsked in my ear. “‘Fairly nice-looking?’ ‘Can you hit anything?’ Seriously? Did you actually just give him the set-up for the Sundance Kid to show off?!” I turned toward her, elated and actually impressed, though she ruined it a little by going on to, “Good Lord, that’s not remotely about baseball.”

“All baseball movies boil down to life and magic,” I said, watching Nate set up his swing. Maybe he was a Sundance. I could use a Sundance or two in my life. “All good movies are arguably—meaning I’ll argue it, just try me, Mary—about life and magic. By which logic, all movies are baseball movies.”

Mary studied me. “Is that you or a Dad quote? Or a Dad-quoting-something-quote?”

“Well,” I said, unable to hide my silly-pleased smile, “it came from somewhere.”

Nikki Thompson
2014 Earl Weaver Baseball Writing Prize Finalist

Dodger Blues

For Liz M.

I. Jackie Robinson

As a child, she didn't think of herself as a girl but as someone who could grow up to play in the Big Leagues. She came from a long line of almost professional baseball players. Naturally she dreamt of sliding into home on national television, of catching carelessly thrown balls at first—stretching those impossible last inches, cleat still on the base, crowd roaring. To overcome her gender's poor confidence, which she mistook for lack of talent, she practiced discipline and repetition with her dad, who played in the minors when there still was a C League. Her ambitions were two generations after her grandpa was drafted by the Milwaukee Brewers, then the U.S. Army. By the end of junior high, she realized she would carry on the family legacy and that gender was predetermined.

II. Pedro Guerrero

She was too thoughtful and too thin and a girl, so she mostly sat on the bench in high school. The boys feared anyone who was smarter than them, and the girls envied anyone who was super-model skinny. At the end-of-season banquet, her softball coach announced her as holding the highest GPA on the team and mentioned a concern for withstanding the playing field's strong winds. He thought he was being funny. Previously, raging at being pulled from the game and mistaking herself for a soccer goalie, she had drop kicked her glove and considered his head. This happened just after she had debated her point over the phone as to why she should get more playing time. For Exhibit A she batted a thousand for two straight games. For Exhibit B she pitched a game of almost perfect innings. Despite dirty softball uniforms and posters of Trent Reznor and Soundgarden hanging in her room, she remained a bookworm and a pariah. Every closing argument she ever made failed against the deafness of preconceptions.

III. Steve Garvey

Years later, she ran into her high school softball coach at the bookstore, and he asked if she had a boyfriend. He was still gray-haired and paunch-bellied and still objectified her wrongly—back then, at pitcher, not first base, even with her long legs and flexibility. Now she would rather have talked softball and why she had to take the blame for the team's errors, since college was teaching her the theory behind boyfriends. She enjoyed being talked about in relation to herself and not as a player on a two-person team. Unable to consistently strike out the side, she had to rely on a team that was indifferent to stopping ground balls, and, as a result trust remained an unknown. With the coach playing the center fielder at shortstop, the catcher at first, and other mismatches, it wasn't really their fault, just as her parent's misery toward each other was learned from her grandparents. Throws to first hurled past even the right field backup, and practice makes perfect, which would have been a good solution, but the obvious is often elusive and self-sufficiency becomes convenient.

IV. Kirk Gibson

The dust of the softball field, the smell of leather gloves, and the salt of cracking sunflower seeds once meant imagining away the outcast at school and the desperate peacemaker at home. Later, the corseted rules of co-ed slow-pitch made the absence of base stealing and the rareness of line drives to the infield more apparent. Now the leather of her cleats was stiff and the soles had forgotten the shape of her feet. Carefully thought-out batting orders were impossible in between the alternating space of man, woman, man. When the bases were awkwardly loaded, women remained the weaker sex, and the intentional walk became an accusation. The rule makers assumed women were less capable at the plate and wrote in the provision for the automatic walk. Remembering her days of real softball, she always took her at bat. The sunflower seeds, which still littered the floor of every dugout, had taken on the bitter of citrus.

V. Dusty Baker

Unlike the rules for being a girl, the rules for softball were clear and written out in a manual somewhere. As a result she was frightened by groups of all women and intimidated by their femininity. Calling off players for fly balls was second nature, but defending herself against the made-up faces of the girls at school was impossible. Because she could back up careless throws and missed grounders, she couldn't understand why girls who she thought were her friends would turn toward their lockers and giggle to a nearby classmate when she said hi in the hallway. These same girls would be as nice as they had to be when they needed help with chemistry homework. She felt more comfortable hanging out with the boys, especially if they were talking sports or cars, but not girls or sex. She took pride in her ponytail disheveled by a batting helmet and understood the way men left the house in old jeans and T-shirts with holes. She learned that other women check the mirror before leaving the house and that softball isn't life.

Anne Colwell

See Me

6:04 PM
Crawling through traffic like a beetle in my black carapace. Alone in my shell. In my rearview, an ambulance, its siren coughing—on and off, on and off—picking one car at a time out of the way, weaving through the mess. It slides by to the left of me, headed where I should already be. I pray for no mistakes tonight. Please God, don't let me miss anything. But I'm already late. And I'll be the only attending.

A song my mother sang comes to me, a Czech lullaby. I whisper-sing the words whose meaning I can't entirely recall. "Hajej, dadej, nynej." Something about little angels. The wash of soft consonants soothes me.

The traffic stops again but the rain picks up, pounding on the roof. I lock out my elbows, push on the steering wheel, will the blue car in front of me forward. The rain slides in sheets down my windshield. Arterial red and venous blue swirl, a blood watercolor, brushed by wipers and spinning ambulance lights. I am alone in my shell.

> THE HENLOPEN TIMES
> *One Night in Your Local ER*
> *Dr. Kriz comes through the door, already running. This is what she'll do all night long, but she's smiling. It's a rainy summer evening at the beach and she knows she'll have a lot of business. I can tell at first glance that she loves what she does; she can't wait to get in there. I introduce myself as a reporter from the* Times *and thank her again for agreeing to let me shadow her tonight. Dr. Kriz buzzes me, along with Ms. Hanner from the public relations department, through the double doors, back to where the action happens. This is the night that I'll find out what it's really like to work in an ER right here in our community, not the TV version we've all seen, but the real thing, in Bayside Hospital, a place most of the readers of* The Henlopen Times *have visited at one time or another.*

6:08 PM

The outside doors fling themselves apart. I'm running. My braid is heavy and wet and I feel its weight pull as I jog through the downpour into the waiting room.

And there he is: the reporter that administration warned me about two weeks ago. Shit. He asked to shadow me, write a piece about the *real* ER, a day in the life, or a night. My life. Tonight. *Hovno.* Shit. I told them to pick another doctor. I told them. I slow my pace, just barely. He reaches out his hand. His hair plastered to his scalp, damp strings on his forehead. He wears a tweedy jacket, soggy, worn at the cuffs. Beside him is that woman from Public Affairs whose name always escapes me. Gwen? Wendy? She's smiling hard.

I take his hand. I grab their elbows. I turn them toward the door I am focused on, the door I have to get through now. "Come with me," I say. "I'm running late."

Gwen/Wendy takes little steps in her clicking heels. "Do you mind if I..."

"Sure. Absolutely." She won't last the night in those shoes.

He's got a recorder gadget and a notepad. He presses a button, says "6:10" and "entering the ER."

Fish and Tancredie are on. Fish passes me headed toward the back bays and pushes a cup of coffee into my hand.

"How did you know?" I say, just as he says, "Where the hell have you been?" He's smiling, and my heart slows a little as I look around. Not too bad. No motor vehicle collisions. No one coding. I take a breath. Wet as I am, the air conditioning goes to my bones.

I look over to the far side of the trauma unit and I scan the plastic chairs for her out of habit. I know even as I do it that it's insane, that I'm disturbed, perseverating. I look at the place where she sat weeks ago, where I held her hand until her friends and family came, until they took her away. She isn't here tonight. She will never be here again. I've been looking every shift for months. Why would she want to sit again in the place where her husband died? What is it that I expect? She'll be here because it is a Friday and he died on a Friday evening? She'll be here because I have willed her to be so many times and somehow... I tell myself that I will stop this. Tonight is the last night that I allow myself this ridiculous indulgence. Done. I'm done.

Her hands were so delicate. She had a straight scar between her thumb and forefinger. I imagined a kitchen accident. I imagined stitching her skin together. Touching her so carefully, slowly.

THE HENLOPEN TIMES

The night shift is just starting. I stand at the desk and wait for Dr. Kriz to get updated before she gives me a tour. Everyone around me moves purposefully; the ER is a hive of worker bees—nurses, technicians, family members, policemen. An orderly passes holding three pizza boxes high over his head and weaving his way toward the break room in the back.

He turns to Dr. Kriz as he passes. "Want a slice?"

"Maybe later," she says.

"It'll go quick," he calls over his shoulder, but Dr. Kriz is already back to work. She is looking at the vital signs on the computer screens and listening while the two doctors who worked the day shift, Dr. John Fisher and Dr. Dan Tancredie, fill her in on the patients in each of the bays.

6:27

I look again at the reporter guy and Gwendy shifting from foot to foot by the desk where I abandoned them like uninvited guests at a crazy party. I raise my finger to them and mouth "one minute" while I listen to Tancredie tell me all about the nursing home patient with chest pain. She was in the ambulance that passed me on the road.

He tells me that she doesn't want tests, that she's refusing treatment. "She says that she's old and she just wants to be left alone to die." Later, when I see her, she is crying. She says that she's been through three C-sections, breast cancer, four surgeries on a broken foot, but she's never been this exhausted in her life. "I'm ready," she says. "I've no one left here. My husband died two years ago. I want to see him again."

I think immediately of Sylvia. My Sylvie. I think of how she held onto the curtain as she stared at her husband's body under the white sheet, just his bruised and shaven head showing. She whispered her name to me when I asked, as though she might wake the man who lay there in front of her. She held her brown hair back in one hand, her knuckles white. Under her lifted arm, I saw the two small holes in the armpit of the threadbare blue tee shirt. Something so intimate about these two holes, so tender. I think of them often. Sylvia is alone in the world, too. I wonder if she's exhausted, if she would let me put my arm around her shoulders the way I'm doing with this woman, lifting her gently.

I have written a script in my head, a made-for-TV romance, awful, in which I come in to work one night and she is waiting here, sitting in that chair where she sat. She is fidgeting, shifting in her seat, leaning forward and pushing her hands through her hair. I am the perfect doctor and woman, and she looks at me full of admiration. I reassure her again that her husband died quickly. A cerebral hemorrhage. That he didn't suffer, that the way the car hit the bike meant it all happened fast. She asks if we could talk more. She says that I've been so comforting. My script is full of holes and we're both caricatures of ourselves, but it's a draft and one I keep reworking.

In the next scene, we are making dinner together in my kitchen, roast pork and root vegetables. She loves the blue and white tiles I've collected from the places I've lived growing up. We listen to Bach's *Cello Suites*, drink Moravian wine, Vino Mikulov St. Laurent. She loves all these things. I can imagine what her laugh might sound like.

If I told Vanessa about this fantasy, what I've been thinking, she'd stop writing, sit forward in her chair, and inspect me over her red reading glasses. I told her once that her "therapist gaze" makes her look like a Sunday school teacher. She would say, "Why do you think that you are attracted to yet another straight woman? Another woman who is unavailable?" This is why I haven't told her. I know what she'd say. Janet in med school. Barbara when I started as an intern at Jefferson. She'd bring them all up again.

As if I didn't see the pattern repeating. As if I could miss my own symptoms.

THE HENLOPEN TIMES

Dr. Kriz asks if I want the penny tour and she walks me around the ER. Bayside is a trauma center, she says, so there are ten beds devoted to the worst kinds of cases, like intestinal bleeding, or car accidents. The four pediatric beds look the same as all of the rest except that the wallpaper around the tops of the bays features Sesame Street characters and alphabet blocks. The other 15 beds are what she calls MAMP, Major Multipurpose—broken arms and legs, the toothache that wakes you in the night, the asthma attack.

Dr. Kriz is a tall sturdy woman, with a long blonde braid and bright, intelligent eyes. She asks if I have questions, and, since we have a moment, I ask her about herself. She graduated from the University of Pennsylvania and Jefferson Medical School. When her parents retired to Lewes, she followed them here to work at the hospital. Her parents were diplomats, she tells me. Her father was the Ambassador to Czechoslovakia at the end of the Cold War. She says she grew up there and all over the world, mostly behind the Iron Curtain. "A diplomat brat," she calls herself.

When I ask her what made her want to be a doctor, she tells me a story about how, as a little girl, she had mysterious stomach pains. She saw many doctors, she says, and they were all so kind. Here Dr. Kriz smiles, "I watched everything they did and I wanted to be just like that." She practiced medicine first on her stuffed animals and dolls, and she dreamed of helping others when she grew up.

I start to ask her why she chose Emergency Medicine, but the police and the EMTs erupt through the doors with a bleeding man strapped to a gurney. "Fell through a window," one of the cops says. The EMT says, "His blood alcohol's through the roof. We couldn't give him much." The man is moaning, in terrible pain.

Dr. Kriz swings into action.

7:27

Everywhere we lived, secrecy and silence. Every city, the dark cars driving past at regular intervals all night, the click and whir every time I picked up the phone. And if my parents missed the curfew, I spent the night alone with the servants. I wondered if anyone I met, I met by chance, or if they were sent. Always eyes. Always ears. My father's warning, "They are watching you, Zsu Zsu. Anyone you talk to might be trying to hurt you."

I had celiac. No one knew what that was then. No one knew that my body was intolerant of what I loved: the dense, marvelous rounds of rye we ate at every meal in Prague; the Vanocka, egg-washed and braided. But I didn't really become a doctor because of the bread. That's the cover story. I became a doctor because of the ballerina. Because of Nela. Such a cliché. Why couldn't she have been a clerk or a housekeeper?

When I was eleven, she lived in my room for three weeks after her husband was shot. She slept on a cot beside my bed and we kept the blinds drawn and she didn't speak because we knew the residence was bugged. Nela wrote on a little white tablet and she cried in the barest whisper into her pillow every night until my father found a way to get her out. She had long dark hair and dark eyes and her feet were fascinating and horrifying, like the hooves of some impossible animal, a unicorn maybe, or a centaur.

Two other men snuck Nela and her dying husband into our house, up through a secret door in the basement. I was the first one to see them coming up from the floor. I started to call out for my father, but his hand came around and clamped over my mouth and he nodded at me and I remembered and I didn't make a sound.

I don't know what Nela's husband had done or why they shot him, but I think now he must have been bleeding out through an artery. His face had that ashen color and he was shivering like he was cold. The doctor came. A gray-haired, rumpled man with pince-nez glasses and full, wet lips. He felt around wounds, shook his head, found the pulse in the man's neck, shook his head again.

All those days, I watched the ballerina move through our house like some silent, long-limbed insect. Thin, so thin, arms and legs like sailor's rope, all those nights sleeping just above her, looking down at her dark head buried in the white pillow, I dreamed of being the one who could bring the bleeding man back. A gift I could give her and she would see me and love me and never forget. I dreamed that my hands could heal by beams of light, by touch, a miraculous power, like the statue of the Infant of Prague.

Everything just-born is covered in blood, eyes of pain and surprise. Maybe everything I ever did after, I did because of that night, that strange birth.

> THE HENLOPEN TIMES
> *Somewhere between the vomiting boy scout, the pool lifeguard with pink eye, and the grandmother with a shoulder dislocation, I slip out for a few minutes to get a cup of coffee. When I sit down in the coffee shop just down the hall from the ER, I realize that I haven't been off my feet since the shift began. I realize, too, that Dr. Kriz has not slipped out, that she and the rest of her heroic team are still standing, still serving.*

9:21

On every shift there's a moment when the whole place takes a deep breath. The noise softens—no phone ringing, no one screaming or calling—and the motion slows. It doesn't last long, but it always comes and I wait for it. I cherish it. Noticing this moment, I am sometimes convinced that there is a pattern in the universe, some kind of music playing that I can't hear, but whoever or whatever has composed it, puts these rests in, even in the most unlikely places.

Then it ends. One of the orderlies erupts into laughter, and, at the same moment, the double doors swing open and the reporter steps through them, already back from the coffee I sent him to get. I hoped he might realize he'd seen enough and go. But here he comes. He stands beside me again, holds the digital recorder between us. He says, "I hate to press, Dr. Kriz, but this is a human interest story, and you're the one the readers are going to be interested in. You're the hero of this story. Do you mind if I ask you some more questions?"

I feel the acid dump into the pit of my stomach. "I am not anyone's hero. I'm not the ER. The story is this place and the whole team, the patients. Not me." He is shaking his head before I finish speaking. Dismissing this. The eyes and ears. His little recorder makes no noise at all. So small he could put it in his pocket if he wanted and no one would know.

He nods toward the empty chairs over near trauma. He takes Sylvie's seat and I sit beside him where I sat with her. I see for just a beat the blue blur of her tee shirt, her lost eyes.

He starts with my parents. "Are they still…around?" So matter of fact. So awful. I tell him they are. I see in my mind their rooms at Cadbury, the assisted care wing, their art crammed on gray walls, my mother's oversized embroidered furniture shoehorned into two rooms. I see her sitting at the kitchen table reading the newspaper through the enlarging lens.

"Could I get in touch with them? Do they live here in Lewes?"

"Yes," I say, "they live in Lewes, and, no, you can't. They have been through enough questioning in their lives." I am pleasant. I am smiling. I show nothing, but he stops writing and looks up at me, not like Vanessa would, but puzzled instead, surprised. I empty my eyes, my expression. I am pleasant and I am nothing. In my shell.

"I'm sorry," he says, and then, "Are you married?"

"No."

"Have you ever been married?"

I haven't thought of Simon in a long time. The poor boy. Always a boy in my mind, though he'd be the same age as me now, fifty-two. I've kept him at twenty-two, suspended like a fossil in the amber of the last evening I ever saw him, loading the boxes into the trunk of his car in the freezing rain. Sometimes I think I'd like to see him again, like the chance to apologize, to explain. There was so much I didn't know then.

"A long time ago," I say. "And too briefly to count."

"So, yes?" he says.

"Okay, yes." He writes on his pad. I try to control my breath. Counting through each one, in and out.

"Kids?"

"No kids." I start to click the pen in the pocket of my lab coat and make myself stop. I wish a wish I never have before—for sirens, for someone bleeding, for anything to stop this.

"So, if you don't mind my asking…" He turns the page on his pad, looks up at me. "Is there someone in your life now?"

To fire a question. I understand for the first time this expression. A bullet.

"Is there someone?" I repeat. It goes through me.

Sylvie grabbing the curtain beside me. Ballistics. Simon standing closing the trunk in the cold rain. "*The initial damage is severe bleeding.*" The textbook in med school. Memorized shards his question pushes out and through. The names of women, the scraps of their conversation I've saved. "*The degree of damage of a projectile is related to the size of the temporary vs. the size of the permanent cavity it creates.*" Nela pushing the bloody body up through the basement floor. My mother at the kitchen table. The song she sang. "Hajej, dadej." My father asking me the same question four times in our last conversation. "*Cavitation is related to yaw, deformation, kinetic energy, fragmentation.*" Does it pass through clean or does it shatter? Will it shatter and tear it all apart? I want to ask him if he knows, if he knows what he's done.

I look at him, but his face is out of focus. A siren in my ears. People are running. "*The greatest danger is the potential for hypovolemic shock.*" I stand up. "*The vital organs receive too little oxygen and begin a cascade of organ failure.*" Someone has called my name.

"No," I say. "No. There is no one."

Then I am moving away.

Carrie Bistline

2014 Frank McCourt Creative Nonfiction Prize Winner

Egress

You still remember the night he said he loved you. Your friend had asked you to dog-sit at her beach house for the weekend. You were into your second bottle of cheap Chardonnay. Andric was chain-smoking and pacing back and forth along the sea-gray deck of the saltwater pool. The air was warm and misty and the way the breeze carried his cigarette smoke away in silver streams made you wish you smoked, too.

He was talking about the military. About rules and survival tactics and life. The first thing they teach you, he said, is to search out the quickest exit when you enter a room. He was leading up to something. You stepped close to him, touched his shoulder to stop him from walking. Your fingers brushed his lips as you slid the cigarette from his mouth.

He lowered his chin and looked you in the eyes as you inhaled. He tilted his head almost imperceptibly and frowned as though he'd just realized something beyond comprehension.

"What?" Smoke swirled out with the word.

"Why do you resist me?"

"I don't trust passion," you said.

"I've lost my point of egress with you."

It was the sweetest thing you had ever heard from a man.

You puffed on the cigarette again. A small inhale this time. It was making you dizzy. Or he was. Or the salt air, or the rasping whisper of the ocean a hundred yards away.

"Maybe you don't need an escape plan," you said.

Two months later, your laptop sits in a box in your sister's basement with a shattered screen and chunks vital to operation missing. Not unlike your life at present. The familiar beep sounds when powering it on. That's a relief. It's the thirty perfectly spaced, monotonously maddening beeps that follow that really push you over the edge.

It broke when his wife threw it. You don't blame her. You didn't know about her, either. If she'd had her laptop within reach, you'd have thrown it, too. Instead, you threw his phone in the toilet while they screamed at one another in the kitchen.

It's then you decide it's a good time to get the fuck out. But you can't get the fuck out without your phone when your sister is twenty hours away by car. Because your sister is the only one to whom you can bear to speak.

"Get the fuck out!" she screams. Word choice. No wonder he loves you both. It's then you realize her wedding ring is gleaming so brightly, brighter than the butcher's knife in her hand.

"I'm just trying to find my phone," you say. Like that is a perfectly normal thing to say when someone is standing in front of you with a butcher's knife.

You do, indeed, get the fuck out after finding your phone under the broken nightstand.

In the following days, you meet Andric's wife, sans butcher's knife, through Facebook. You learn you'd been living with a man who'd given you a fake last name. He's a recovering alcoholic and a liar, she says.

"You're his seventh affair in an eight-year marriage," she says, before you cut off communication with her because she won't stop messaging you.

A whole week you make him beg from afar. And like the perfect other woman, you return as his mistress. He has two more months on his job in this town, and you plan to go with him to the next town. The accusation from his wife that you are just another girl in another town is absurd. No one knows him as you do. You are the one he really loves. To your arms he'd been forced by her rigidity. To your warmth he'd flown from her coldness, her indifference. It was the first time he'd ever truly felt love. He couldn't tell you about the wife he'd been planning to divorce for years, because he knew he'd lose you.

After you come back, you make him explain away his lies. Some make sense, some don't. Some you will yourself to believe. Some you forgive. Some you can't. And those you bring up every night.

"Did you think you could go through an entire divorce without me ever finding out about her?" you ask again.

"I hoped so," he says without looking away. Because he never looks away.

"How could you hide something like that? How could you take that choice from me?"

He leans in and places his rough hands on either side of your face. God, you love those hands. "My only concern, in all of this, has always been you. From the first moment I met you, I had to have you. I didn't care what it took. It wouldn't matter if I had a girlfriend, a mistress, or five wives. It wouldn't matter who I hurt to keep you, as long as you were safe with me," he says.

You drop the subject and go take a bath. You hear the kitchen freezer door open, glass clink, and a thud as the door shuts again. You didn't want to drink tonight, but you'll have to now, if you don't want to be the sober one listening to the drunk guy. He takes three double-shots of Crown and the result is a coin toss. Some nights, a tsunami full of remorse and regret pummels him and he cannot seem to find solid ground again. He takes another shot, and you give up trying to match him shot for shot. Still, he pours another, trying to drown out the flood, and he talks until he cries, and you give up and go to bed, leaving him cooking for himself in the kitchen because you both had skipped dinner.

Other nights, he cannot take his eyes or hands off of you. He tells you how much he loves you, how much he needs you. These nights, you drink together. You are careful to always make his drinks for him, so you can control the tsunami. And you talk and laugh together. You kiss, you touch, you sit on his lap like a spoiled child. And then sing and dance to "Crash Into Me" with Dave Matthews.

When you wake with a hangover on a Tuesday, you think, again, that drinking like that on a weekday has to end. Drinking like that on any day has got to end. You call him at work and tell him so, and he agrees. He comes home for his lunch break and you make love like you hadn't seen each other six hours ago.

From the bedroom that night, you hear a thud and glass clink. You walk into the kitchen, where Andric is standing with the refrigerator door open, scanning the shelves. You go back to the bedroom to continue folding clothes. A few moments later, you hear the clink again. This time, you walk into the kitchen in time to see him shutting the freezer door and wiping his mouth with the back of his hand.

Weeks after your return, you get an email from his wife with a picture of her call log from her phone. There are several long phone calls to and from Andric.

According to him, they are getting a divorce and speak only through lawyers. You tell him you understand if they need to speak, that you just want him to be honest about it. The way you tell a child with chocolate on his face, "You won't be in trouble if you just tell me now that you ate the candy." He denies all contact. He's adamant. He calls her in front of you and tells her to leave you both alone. Before she can respond, he hangs up and throws the phone.

"She'll do anything to get you away from me," he says as he holds you to his broad chest.

You hack into his phone records after a few days. You research his name, his family, his friends. You realize you've known all along. Your family begged you not to go back. Your friends have stopped checking on you. You feel a guilt you can't quite place every time you call your sister. She knows. She knows, and she is waiting for you to admit that you know. That you know your lying, alcoholic, married boyfriend isn't the exception to the rule.

You finally find your point of egress. You pack boxes of belongings while he's at work. You meet him for lunch, then stop at the post office to send the things to your sister's house 1,300 miles north.

He's surprised when you pour him a drink before he sits his briefcase down that night. You drink, cook, and laugh together.

"What's wrong?" he says.

"Nothing," you lie. You stare at him. You know he can see everything you're thinking. Your thoughts are written as clearly as the letter he'd given you after the housesitting weekend—scrawled on yellow-lined paper and signed with, "P.S. Passion is a good thing."

"Would you tell me if you needed something?" he asks.

"Yes," you say. You want him to stop you.

"You left your email up. Why did your sister send you money?"

You look down. You've never been good at lying. "She knows I haven't been working. She's worried."

You run to the car in the rain, and he opens the door for you. You bring the frozen yogurt home. You make love. You make love again, and you cry yourself to sleep.

You pack your car the next morning and leave what won't fit. You're torn about the Smith and Wesson 9 millimeter he'd given you. It isn't registered. Taking it seems wrong. But leaving it says too much. You leave it. You leave it with the bathrobe, the lamp made from soldered horseshoes, and the black down comforter you won't be able to sleep under alone.

Earlier that morning, you had grabbed his hand as he walked out the door. You slipped into his arms and pressed your body against his chest. He ran his hands firmly down both sides of your spine.

You'd kissed him softly and lied, "I'll see you tonight."

Laurie Ann Guerrero

Casketing

I've buried everything I've ever loved
in the bone of reason: now, even in dreams
you are dead. Sometimes, I wheel your metal-
colored coffin to the grocery store.
Once, to a paperie. Twice to Fiesta
Bakery on Pleasanton. You are heavy.
Once, I was in high school, in a play, and parked
you stage left. Always, I shake you: Wake up,
damn you. Sometimes, the casket is open
and I kick you. And when, in my small shoes, I
make contact, your ribs crumble like the bark
of an old mesquite: wake up, wake up! We can't
run the numbers, argue, make your mother's bread
if you are always going to be dead.

Laurie Ann Guerrero

Untouchable

If you are always going to be dead
who then will melt away the breasts from my
chest? Need more my eyes than the unraveling
of my hips? In your house, I was all elbows
and teeth. A stopped clock—just as much man as
woman. Or rain. You were blind and I loved
you for it. In your house, my shoulders grew
to fit the work, patience blossomed upon
my head: a crown. You were my mirror: my name,
ready plum of my right hand, my ancient
and river'd neck, my compass, my wing, my
open gate, my warrior, my sleepless legion—
as if I had been born male: my kingdom come.
And one day in hot July, my kingdom gone.

Mary Miller:
The *Cobalt* Interview

Mary Miller is the author of a story collection, *Big World,* and a novel, *The Last Days of California.* Her work has appeared in *McSweeney's Quarterly, New Stories from the South, American Short Fiction, Mississippi Review,* and others. She currently serves as the John and Renee Grisham Writer in Residence at Ole Miss.

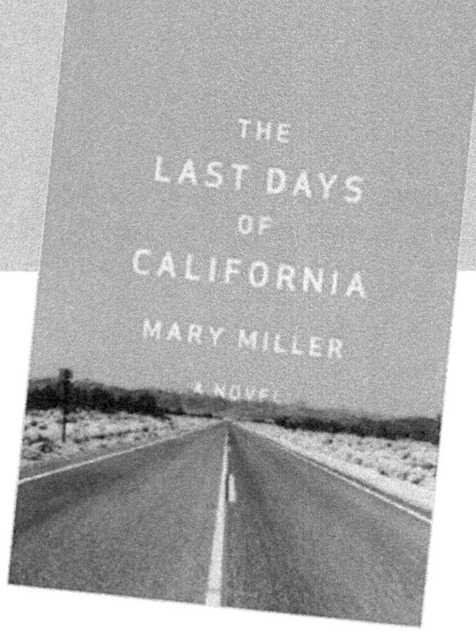

by Andrew Keating

Mary Miller
The *Cobalt* Interview

Andrew Keating: I'd like to begin with an identity question. You mention in the acknowledgments of your first novel, *The Last Days of California*, that you previously considered yourself "always and only" a short story writer. Can you first tell me a little about what this means and how you initially came to that decision?

Mary Miller: I love short stories. I love being able to switch gears and write about whatever I want to write about at the moment. A novel is such a huge commitment and commitments have never really been my strong suit. You have to live inside a novel, be totally dedicated to it, and that's difficult. You also have to be willing to shut everything else out. *The Last Days of California* is the only novel-length story I've started that I felt compelled to finish (and it's a pretty short novel).

AK: How did the transformation to writing a novel come about, and what were some of the key differences in the process of writing The Last Days of California from your work in short stories?

MM: Though I never intended to write a novel, I've always been of the opinion that every story tells you how long it wants to be and you have to listen. Only ten or so pages into *The Last Days*, I felt obligated to these characters. And then there came a point at which I simply couldn't give up on them. When I wasn't working on it, I felt like I was letting this family down—they had somewhere to go, there was a trajectory I'd set in motion—and I couldn't stop until their story had been told.

As far as the difference in process, I definitely thought more about plot and tension. I wanted people to keep turning pages, page after page, which I don't think about when writing short stories. With a short story, you can get away with very little action; if it's done well, characters can just sit around a bedroom or a kitchen and talk. You can't get away with that in a novel. It's sort of like the novel that takes place solely inside one person's head. Rarely does this turn out well or see the light of day.

AK: Well, now you've done it. The novel is complete and out there in the world, and it has been well-received. Is this something you think you'll do again in the near future? Or is it back to short stories?

MM: I'd love to be a long-form writer and call myself a novelist, but I'm not and I don't. I still consider myself a short story writer, though I'm not ruling out another novel. More and more, novellas are beginning to seem like a very good idea. Why is the novella so despised, unpublishable? Mostly, though, I try not to think about length too much—a great story can be three hundred words or three hundred thousand and both are difficult.

AK: *The Last Days of California* seems to be a story about faith. Faith is an important piece of southern culture. Are you religious, or do you come from a religious family? (If so, how did your own experience with faith factor into the writing of this novel?)

MM: I am religious, though I'm not practicing anymore. I grew up in a strict Catholic household. My siblings and I were told that Catholicism was "the one true religion" and this always bothered me. I remember asking our mother questions: What if I had been born in China or India? What if everyone believes that *theirs* is the "one true religion?" But for a long time I didn't question her assessment of Catholicism with much enthusiasm; I didn't think about it too much.

While writing *The Last Days*, I put myself in Jess's shoes. What if my father had been taken our family on a cross-country trip like this? What if I'd *had* to question what we were doing and why? Jess is forced to confront her beliefs in a way that most of us aren't, at least not at fifteen.

AK: Your narrator, Jess, wants to believe, her sister doesn't really care (perhaps representing what Jess's youth could be: fun, uninhibited, but not without consequences), her father gives up on his pilgrimage for the allure of a casino, and it becomes clear that Jess's mother is the only character with unwavering faith (but that faith appears to be in her husband more than in God). How much of this was developed prior to sitting down to write?

MM: Very little was developed early on, basically nothing. When I began writing, I knew there were four characters in a Waffle House and they were on their way to California to await the rapture. So I knew the basic premise, but little else. I didn't know who they were, what they believed, what they wanted. I never want to know too much beforehand, or think about what I'm doing too much. If the author already knows where she wants to take you, where she wants to go, it feels inauthentic, forced. I write in order to learn.

While writing the first draft, I would often find myself thinking about these characters and their journey. They became very real to me. I guess I'm saying that I did more "plotting" than I realize.

AK: The nearing rapture creates urgency for the characters in *Last Days*. What were your intentions in demonstrating the different effects that such this type urgency can have on people?

MM: Oh, that's a good question. As far as writing, the nearing rapture provided me with momentum and a guide. And for the characters, each of them had to confront themselves in a way that they would never have to do at home. They're uncomfortable and hot and stuck together in cars and crappy motel rooms. They're on this trip together as well as individually, and each of them is dealing with unique stressors.

AK: Everything I read about you categorizes you as a *writer of the South*. I'm curious if you see yourself in this way—as a writer who is distinctly from the South–and, if so, what it means to be a *writer of the South*, exactly?

MM: I'm a Southerner, and if I'm labeled as such that's fine with me. In interviews and reviews, it's mostly my fellow Southerners who label me this way, which is sort of nice; they want to claim me. But I don't particularly think of myself in any way, other than a writer, and sometimes I don't even feel like that. I guess it depends on how much actual writing I've been doing.

AK: At the time of this interview, you're nearing the end of your first semester of a teaching appointment at Ole Miss. How is that going? What lessons are you taking from being on that side of the workshop?

MM: It's going really well. I'm teaching a graduate fiction workshop and my students are incredibly hard working, smart, and dedicated. I leave (almost) every class feeling really great about what I'm doing, what they're doing. I couldn't be more pleased, really.

One thing that's been difficult is that sometimes I forget I'm not a student. I get so caught up in the discussion that I want to join in as if I'm one of them. I guess I still consider myself one of them. I think this is pretty typical. I think of my professors as the *real professors* and they probably think of their professors as the *real* ones. So you have to go back to the very beginning, wherever that is, to find the really real one.

AK: Something I always want to ask authors about—but rarely do—is failure. Are there any recent projects that you've just *loved* on a concept level but never worked out?

MM: Oh, gosh, so many stories don't work out. I tried to write a number of novels before *The Last Days of California* and they were all bad—floundering, pointless. One thing that's pretty great, though, is this: if I have a story I really want to tell and keep searching for the right way to tell it, it usually happens, eventually.

AK: Mary, this has been great. Thank you for taking the time to speak with us. As we wrap up, I feel it necessary to ask: What's next?

MM: At this point, I'm not sure what's next. I'm writing most days and I just want to keep it up; I want to love it again. I think a lot of us go through phases where writing simply isn't fun and it seems like no one cares anyway and we forget why we do it. That whole *I write because I have to* thing, well, I don't feel this way ninety-nine percent of the time. I'd rather watch a movie or go to Planet Fitness or hang out with some dogs. I dream about what else I might do—some other line of work—like maybe I could be an EMT or work at a home for abused children? I'm not trying to be coy, I just feel weird about talking about stories that may not work out right now.

D. Watkins

Class Trip

East Baltimore is my home—murder's the stench mixed with smoke from the pistols that continuously bang over twenty-four hour sirens. Baptist churches, Korean stores and teenage dope-dealers own the corners. Dope fiends are mentors. Grandmas are thirty and pregnant. Automatic weapons are accessorized with multicolored Nikes, no one graduates from anything, all the whites are cops or teachers, black life expectancy is sixteen if you're lucky, and the primary causes of death are dice games, diabetes and drug overdoses.

My friend Taja, little brother Deion and I are walking to school.

A black Honda is sitting on the corner of Fayette Street. The tags are paper and the windows are cracked, a wisp of smoke floats out. The passengers see us and then pull off.

"Yo, you don't get no pussy! I'm fuckin sumthin like POW POW POW after school. Bet!" yells Taja. Taja's tall with a tall face—I ignore him like I always do while damping my index in saliva and de-crusting Deion's face because even at age seven, he still cries and snots every hour on the hour.

Deion snaps and pulls away with heavy eyes. He is mad that Taja, me and the rest of the seventh grade are going on a trip to the Smithsonian Museum in D.C. He wanted to tag along, and I normally let him come everywhere with me—to the dirt bike trails at Bocek's where I hone my stunts, to run and jump the gates with me after hours at Patterson Park pool, to teenage house parties with my lusty pants-rubbing friends, to every basketball game I ever played in and anywhere else, but today is out of my hands.

Taja and I had been talking about this trip for months. We both watched *Jurassic Park* sixty plus times. Had flipped over the way the raptors had flossed with Samuel L. Jackson's bones. We couldn't wait to see the real thing, or at least their fossils anyway.

•

A block and a half away from the school and we are a half hour early, which is great for kids like us who normally arrive around second period. I hope I sit next to Tarsha Jackson on the bus. Last year we took a bus trip to Fort McHenry, and she let me stick my hand up her skirt. She blanketed our legs with my Soda Club jacket, and then I poked half of my index in her and spun it around like a tornado while her fat friend Karen watched with a disapproving smirk. The smirk grew when I placed my finger next to Karen's nose to smell.

"I'm sittin by that freak bitch Tarsha Jackson," yells Taja aimlessly, walking into oncoming traffic. "Yo, pay attention. You almost got hit!" I shout, pulling him back to the curb.

That same black Honda rides through the light, skimming us, and then slams on the brakes. I yank Taja away just in time. A twenty-something in a skullcap and Timb boots hops out from the passenger side.

"Lil mans, y'all aight?" he asks, looking left and right. His skin is the color of dark liquor, it's mostly covered by an oversized army jacket with linted Velcro.

"Yeah, we good," I reply. "We got school."

"Cool, lil mans. Y'all get in the car," the dude says. His forehead slopes over his eyes and he sounds like he smokes way too much.

"Naw, our school right there," Taja answers, with a little extra base in his voice.

Dude shows us a pistol peeking out of his waist and insists, "Get in the fuckin car. Don't make a scene yo."

He guides the three of us into the back of the Honda. It smells like Newports and an oil change. The back seat and floor is covered with smashed cigarette boxes, Twinkie wrappers, blunt guts and empty Hennessey bottles. Deion is about to cry in 3... 2...

"Don't cry, Deion. We gonna be okay," I whisper while squeezing his trembling palm.

•

We ride past Ellwood Park and over the bridge on Eager by some boarded up homes and then the driver stops. My heart swells; I feel it pumping through three layers of clothes. The driver has yet to turn around. We face his back. I wonder what he sounds like, do we know him? The forehead guy spins around, cocking his hammer—not the one on his waist, but another that's wrapped in a plastic Super Fresh bag. He brushes all of our small noses with the tip, it crinkles when it reaches mine. I see the imprint of the gun through the blue plastic. It looks like a Desert Eagle. "Yo, I know you Sean Moe son. I know you got the house key. I know he in there. Kick it out!" he says. Taja is Sean Moe's son—they even wear the same face. Sean Moe sells crack with my father. He's tall, lanky and towers like the eleven story project building that he and my dad hustle out of. The building we live in. Everyone knows Sean Moe—he dresses in nothing but leather and suede and diamonds, he only drives Mercedes, and not the little cheap C and E class, but the CL or SL. He and my dad are best friends, they're inseparable, they always brag about how they make each other rich; sometimes they get drunk and make me and Taja wrestle to see who has the toughest son.

"I ain't gonna kill y'all if y'all do what I say!" He looks at Taja with his hand out. Taja reaches for his keys and squeaks, "You ain't gonna hurt my dad, is you?"

"Naw, shorty chill," says the guy. "I'm a go holla at Sean right quick and we gone let ya'll go to school," he looks at the driver, "Yo if they try hop out, kill'em." The driver doesn't respond, he just nods. Our eyes well up at the notion, Taja's overflow first. I catch Deion's before they trickle, squeezing his hands tighter—his flesh reddens. I want to cry too.

I'm beyond scared, we all are. We'll probably die. Kids get dumped in dumpsters and tossed behind buildings all of the time. I see it on TV, I hear it in music, some of my friends are dead and my older brother talks murder daily.

I hope they don't toss us, I hope they don't kill Deion, I hope our family finds us if they do, and we're not like those missing kids they hang on the posters in the market.

I want to scream, but I have to be strong for Deion. If I lose it, he'll lose it. Snot bubbles are foaming around Taja's nostrils, his face is drenched. Taja's all bark, he tries to act gangsta like his pops, but secretly loves Power Rangers more than Deion. Sean Moe makes Taja wear Hilfiger, Polo and Nike, and he proudly accepts it to impress his dad, but Taja prefers Red Ranger t-shirts and doesn't care about fresh sneakers or drugs or sex. Taja likes being a kid.

•

They whip the car around to the top of Sean Moe's block—a row house not far from our school. The dude hops out—gun in hand—and runs toward Sean Moe's crib. The driver cuts on Wu Tang and sparks a cig. M.E.T.H.O.D. Mannnnnnnn bumps out his flat speakers with no bass. I can smell, hear and taste our anxiety—the driver's anxiety too. He cracks a Hennessy bottle and takes a huge swig. I wipe Deion's tears on my hoodie, I'm so proud of him for not screaming—Taja is a wet statue. His fumes have fogged up the back window as he wept. The driver turns up Method Man.

The dude is jogging back up the street, five minutes or so have passed. He jumps back into the Honda.

"Done. Drop them off at the top of the block yo," he tells the driver while reaching for the Hennessey. The driver shifts the car into gear, "Hold up!" the passenger says. He opens the car door and throws the gun into the sewer hole. "Now drive." We were next I thought. Taja's shaking more than Deion, I'm envisioning my own death. I think I'm ready. I squeeze my eyes tight, so tight that my brain cringes.

•

"Listen! I want y'all to run up the alley to the end of the block and don't turn round. When you get there, take Madison and walk ya little asses to school. Don't say shit. If I hear police or think that y'all tryin to be slick," he said with jiggly cheeks and spit raining on us, "I'ma kill all of y'all. Now go, run!"

The car stops, we fling the door open, exit and hard-ass like Olympic runners up the alley, past fiends, through mounds of trash towards Madison. Deion falls, his book bag hits the ground and empty pages scatter. His hands are scraped and bloody. I help him up, and we keep booking—Taja, twenty-five lengths in front of us—never stops. The three of us breathe like asthma patients once we reach the peak of the block.

"Should we—should we walk to school now?" Taja pants, both hands on his knees. I cover Deion's ears, "Naw we need to go check on your dad."

•

We drop Deion off with my mom and walk back over to Sean Moe's block. The entire hood is out; yellow tape separates them from the crib. Cop uniforms are strong-arming a bunch of shouting-ebony faces, with Taja's stepmother in the center of it all screaming.

"WHY! WHY!"

Taja's knees hit the concrete. I cover his face with my coat. I don't want him to see the ambulance workers bring Sean Moe out on a stretcher. I muffle his coughs and sniffs as they walk Sean Moe's lifeless body down the steps. His left arm dangles over the edge of the stretcher—his invisible diamonds glaring off the mourning black faces in the crowd.

Two plainclothes cops snatch Taja's stepmom—probably homicide. Her satin robe is blood-pinkish and barely covers her bottom half. She doesn't care. She just witnessed her husband's murder.

I use all of my strength to pull Taja away from the scene.

Kate Wyer

The newest title available from Cobalt Press

excerpt from *Black Krim*

From my window I watch the old man turn circles in the field. There is snow, not much, but enough to cover the ground. He is barefoot and walking with his head down, a single dark figure against the declining light.

I let the curtain fall back against the sill and move toward the phone, but instead of calling anyone, I return to the window again. The man is still circling. I pull on my gloves, my coat, my boots and now move toward him without hesitation.

He looks up at me and stops walking. The cold shakes him.

"Come with me," I say. I offer my gloved hand. He reaches for it, takes it. He is silent. He trips a little, his feet red and stiff, the bones bold struts.

"Keep your head down, out of the wind," I tell him, and I rub his large hand between my small ones. He smiles in a childish way. He listens, ducks into the wind and shelters his face. His large ears are red, his lips blue. His balding scalp shines.

We cross the field, the street, the front yard. The dogs jump at him as he crosses the threshold.

"Get down, Macie!" he says and pulls his arms up into his body, away from the excited animals. His voice is louder than I expected.

"That's Blue and that's Wilson," I say and look into his face.

"I don't have a Macie."

The old man laughs. He stands in the doorway looking down at his feet. The dogs lick the water pooling on the floor from his wet hems. They take big snorting breaths of him and then, tails still wagging, leave the room. I give him a large towel and he wipes his face and head, dries his hands and then drops it to the floor. He uses his left foot to cover the right with the towel, rubs it dry, then shifts feet and dries the other the same way. He looks up at me, waiting.

"Come sit down." I gesture toward the kitchen. He leaves the towel on the floor, follows me. The old man pulls out a chair at the table and sits down, places his hands on the tablecloth, palms up. He stares at the redness of his fingers. A thin clear light catches in the fluid collecting in the rim of his nostril. His face confirms what I thought from the window. He doesn't know where he is, what he was doing out there.

"What's your name?" I ask and lean into the doorframe.

He wipes his nose with his sleeve, but he doesn't respond.

"Where do you live?" I try.

He looks like a child who knows violence, who knows how to avoid it. He shrugs, a slight lifting of the shoulders, and then rubs his palms together. They make a dry scraping sound, like when a window opens after a long cold spell.

I put water on for coffee and then leave to see what clothing I have to fit him; the strangeness of the situation starting to become more real, now that the immediate danger from the cold is over. I dig through my old dresser, pause to push the hair out of my face and then pull it back into a ponytail. Sweatpants, old and with busted elastic, will have to do. I drape them over my neck and then run water in the tub until it becomes warm. There is a dried out palm tree in a blue ceramic pot in the corner of the bathroom. It came with the house, with the previous owner's lack of attention. The pot looks big enough to hold the man's feet, bigger than any bowl I have. I tip it over, grab the trunk of the tree, thump it out of the container and leave it all—the dirt, the root ball, the plant—on the tile. I fill the pot with water a few times, swirling out the remaining dirt, and then carry it downstairs.

The old man startles when I return.

I put the pot on the floor. "I got you these," I say and hand him the pants.

He stands, loosens his belt and drops his jeans. I turn my back to him quickly, surprised.

He taps me on the shoulder to tell me that he's finished changing and then hands me his wet jeans. The sweatpants are tight on him and come to about mid-calf. He does a half-squat to try to stretch them a little and then sits back in the chair, eases his feet into the warm water.

I feel the jean pockets for a wallet and don't find one.

"You lost your wallet?"

"No, I don't believe so."

"It's not in your pants. Is it in your shirt pocket?"

He feels the front pockets of his flannel and shakes his head.

"You musta taken it already." He doesn't seem concerned.

My hair is wet at the temples from the snow, my nerves, and the effort to bring the man in from the cold. I rub my sleeve against my head to dry the dampness and then throw his pants down the stairs to the basement, to put them in the dryer after he's settled.

I start to respond, then stop. The coffee pot finishes its cycle; it hisses and bubbles the last of the water.

"You should have something warm to drink."

The man shakes his head no, reconsiders, then nods yes. I pour two cups and place one in front of him.

"I have milk, not cream. Do you want some? And brown sugar—that's the only kind I have."

"Yes, that's fine with me." I add the milk and brown sugar, place a spoon into the mug.

"Who can I call to come get you?"

He moves his feet in the bowl, shifts them slightly. A small wave passes over the lip onto the floor. The dogs come back into the room and then settle near my feet as I stand at the counter.

I should call the cops, I think. He has slumped a little, his coloring closer to healthy. The warmth of the water and the room are making him sleepy. I've never known an elderly man. No grandfathers, no father. No uncles, no older brothers. I study his long eyebrows, his white stubble, and the lines around his mouth.

He is still silent. *Does he even have anyone to call? What if he doesn't—if he's homeless?*

I walk up the stairs to the spare bedroom. I've never changed the sheets, never needed to. The room is one I imagined filling when I bought the house. I imagined company. I turn around in the room, seeing it again, looking at it with a stranger's eyes. A mirror and a dresser from a yard sale. A framed print of some feathers blowing down the beach. Striped wallpaper in light grays and blues. A few clumps of dog hair by the baseboards. I turn on the bedside lamp.

He'll be more together after some sleep.

I call to him from the top of the stairs. "You should lie down. I have the guest room ready."

I hear him remove his feet from the bowl and then the grunt as he walks back to the hallway to get the towel he left there. The dogs' chains shake as they too get up. He stands at the foot of the stairs, puts his hand on the railing.

"Thank you," he says and concentrates on the steps. I wait for him at the top and then move aside to push the door open a little more. He nods, closes the door behind him. The bed takes his weight and the light clicks out. I stand there a moment longer in the dark hallway, hear his strange breaths.

Éireann Lorsung
2014 Gabriela Mistral Prize Finalist

Kingfishers

One feather, a
gleam of oil,

equals waiting
for long evenings.

The blue dark.
I made new

meaning when meaning
didn't fit my

desires. I said,
fish is fish;

the water, rumpled
with bird, is

water. I see
now birds are

stars. Your hands,
one more universe.

Rain. Something green
flies across, shining.

No list of names for all things.

Éireann Lorsung

Gone

When the storm came
it was already too late.

In 1977 you are born
and your father stays

six months in hospital.
Say the words

electroconvulsive therapy
and wind shears buds

from the weeping birch.
Clear path from cause

to effect. Hailstones
and insurance claims.

Gale-strength
wind and the loss

of consent—
———————.

Memory is control
over the past.

And now they write
the treatment

has no effect on schizophrenia—
I am trying to understand

love that loses itself
in emptiness,

how something without substance
changes daily life.

Air itself is nothing
until it takes the roof away.

Éireann Lorsung

Bramble

Five-petaled, milkwhite, meaning
thin as milk, but less wholesome:

centers that pulp
in July. All year their stems

overrun gardens, paths, empty
lots. Bramble a lesson

in economy. Give nothing
away. Beget. My England consisted

of bramble: rain in bus
shelters, the taste of salt stepping

off a train. An estuary in the morning
mistaken for a vow. A nothing

I survived on, barely.
I scraped, every chance I got.

Bunkers overgrown with blackberries.
The last time I was a girl.

Jen McGuire

Falling in Love through Van Morrison

If you have dated my boyfriend, then you have imagined dancing with him at your wedding to a Van Morrison song. When I first fell in love with Colin one sweet, hot New York summer at the end of my 20's, I imagined we would dance our first dance at our wedding to "And It Stoned Me" from *Moondance*, in spite of the fact that the story of the song has nothing to do with romantic love.

So forgetting I'd never really wanted a wedding and willfully ignoring most of the lyrics, I pictured myself singing "stoned me just like goin' home" up at Colin's bearded face and swaying against him with our friends and families vague and low-lit around us. An old girlfriend of Colin's wrote that she used to imagine they would play "Caravan" to end their wedding. "Caravan" is also on *Moondance*. Only two slim songs separate hers and mine on the album, dangerously proximate, but she claims she would have gone with the version from *The Last Waltz*, that fabulously, deviously Robbie Robertson-heavy, drugged-out Scorsese documentary about the break-up of The Band in which Van is one of the featured guests.

I know Colin would never have agreed to feature that recording of this song at his wedding. Because it's ghastly up-tempo, coke-slurred, and strained. There's no subtlety in it, little feeling beyond that which accompanies ego, so unlike the controlled passion in the studio recording, its aggression outdone only by the sequined purple leisure suit Van is wearing while he struts through the performance. The best thing about the video clip is not Van's vocals, but how hot Robbie is on his guitar. It was 1976. A lot was going wrong.

And since it is the mystic timelessness of Van's writing that keeps its claim on Colin, it is perfectly understandable that he would have scoffed that girl's desire to end their phantom wedding with *The Last Waltz,* "Caravan," into an embarrassed nothingness, had she expressed it to him at the time.

•

Colin followed his father to Van. In the evenings when he was a teenager, his dad had taken to secluding himself in the dining room while the rest of the family, his three sons and wife, watched TV or did homework in the living room. Among the music that drifted out with the cigarette smoke to fog up this fatherless, small-town tableau—Dylan, The Band, and Van Morrison.

•

On his mask, Colin is a cynic. There are ways to see behind it. Hurting him is one way. There are others. I knew him a little in undergrad. Eleven years later and over six years ago, we met for a drink as two single people, talked for seven hours, mostly about politics, shared a kiss on a stoop next to the bar, and started seeing each other.

The first time I went to his apartment on Manhattan's Upper East Side, he had invited me over to cook dinner together and to listen to some of his "phenomenal" taste in music. We ended up ordering from a local vegan place. And he didn't play Van that first night. Instead he played Joni Mitchell, Dylan, and Ani, introduced me to the yearning indie rock poetry of Okkervil River, and inexplicably freaked me out with a child's rendition of "Desperado" from the Langley Schools Music Project that left me racing around the living room in attempt to calm my increasingly rabbit-like heartbeat. I remember him watching me quietly, perplexed and amused, from the stained cream-colored pillow he sat on to smoke comfortably out the fifth floor window. I remember how the approach to each kiss felt like the truest slow-motion movie moment of my life.

It couldn't have been easier for me to fall in love with him. He was smart and passionate, a little arrogant, broad-shouldered, had a great beard, and generously, eagerly shared with me what he loved. The music he loved.

•

For a long time, I had a picture in my head of what a display of passion should look like. There was a hazy frenzy about this image, which I may have blurred together from a childhood of 80s movies, in the standard I set for the level of freedom it would take to let myself really dance or enjoy music in front of other people. Tiny phenomena, made monstrous, powered by a joy I learned long ago not to show, or eventually, to feel. I remain strangely fixated on conceptions—and displays—of happiness. My mind flashes on over-exposed pictures of myself, or other people, laughing wildly, grinning, crying out in unashamed pleasure. A cinema of derangement playing over in my brain, inspired by all those blond women in John

Hughes movies whooping, intimidatingly eager for sex with James Spader or a ride in a convertible or a date to the prom. What vertiginous pleasures, death-defying stunts I could not dare to perform myself. Stories up, teetering on the tightrope or dangling from a trapeze, trapped inside a faraway loneliness and sweating through the suspicion that I was not mechanically capable of falling terribly, painfully in love like everybody else. Because to fall, heaven help me, you have to be able to let go.

•

Van has a couple of hit songs that get played on commercial radio or featured in Julia Roberts movies. Colin feels that to enjoy "Brown Eyed Girl" or "Moondance," say, neither of which I have any particular objection to, would cheapen him, would compromise his appreciation of Van's visionary brilliance. Van, *Van Morrison*, Colin's Northern Irish shaman, lumped in with One Hit Wonders by people who know two overplayed songs from weddings and the oldies station. As Colin preaches, Van the Man is so much more than that.

Van is a poet and a soul-seeker, a troubadour who *loves to love the love that loves to love*. His lyrics are stunning, enveloping, unending. They come from God. Listen to his stuff. I swear he's staring straight into the sun as he writes. And beyond the words, there is that ecstatic, soaring reach in his voice. It calls you closer and then hurtles you to the sky. You find yourself inside it. And by the time you realize you've been lured all the way into his pain, you've been pulled straight through to the other side of your own. What glory. In his famous review of *Astral Weeks*, Lester Bangs writes that "much of the feeling [in Van's music] comes from the reaching." And as Colin says, "Babe, I mean, come on. *Who sings like that*?"

But if he could have predicted he'd end up so misunderstood, supernatural genius notwithstanding, I suspect Van would have ended it all before he'd begun. He's not known as a performer who enjoys his audience. There are those stories of him singing with his eyes closed or his back to the crowd. And he doesn't strive to be transparent or accessible with his writing. As he told Rolling Stone, "I'm not surprised people get different meanings out of my songs. But I don't want to give the impression that I know what everything means 'cause I don't… There are times when I'm mystified." I've often wondered—seeing the audience, reaching out toward them with his words, could it be a distraction from this fascinating *into the mystic* source he connects with when he makes music?

•

I don't remember the first time Colin played Van for me. I remember later, as spring became summer, when we were already singing along to *Moondance* during late nights on the fire escape. If I listen for it, if I tune my ear to the back-then, I can actually hear my own happiness. It doesn't sound explosive and fevered. It's quieter, more delicate, a soothing white noise that helps me ungrip my heart. The fan whirs, blowing the smoke out the window, letting us inhale and exhale only conversation, Colin's deep voice like a levee, resolute and shielding against the New York City nights. We played so much music that was new to me, but when I listen to those beginning days, I hear only Van, and he is singing just one song—"And It Stoned Me."

See, when we kissed on the stoop the night we met for a drink, before the first night at his place, a cliché had snaked up through my gut and my heart and into my head. I was sitting on his right side, he had a cigarette in his left hand and, against all city ordinances, a beer on the step below us. It was a cool April night. He had asked me twice if I wanted to bring my jacket outside before we slid off our barstools, and I remember I told him, arch and playful, that I could definitely manage my own temperature regulation. Outside he kissed me and while he was kissing me and I was kissing him, I thought, terribly unoriginally, "I feel like I've come home."

A month or two later, he played me *Moondance*. He likes to introduce people to Van with this album. His copy of the CD had been lent out so often that by the time it made its way to me, it was badly scratched. The first six songs played okay, though, so I would listen to them over and over again. When I heard the lines, "And it stoned me to my soul / Stoned me just like goin' home," something real, a deep imprint, hearkened back to that first kiss. "And It Stoned Me" became a trigger for me, a permission slip of sorts, to be unbound and unafraid, to be free to fall in love.

And, surely, by a similar force, when he hears Van's music, Colin is pulled back to his father. Not consciously; it must be more elemental than that. But with lyrics like "Hear your children singin' / My Daddy's comin' home" on "Old Old Woodstock" on *Tupelo Honey*, however could it be otherwise? Although he insists his love of Van has nothing to do with his father—the father who introduced him to Van, who threw him a ball and took him fishing and taught him the value of ideas, the father from whom the growing distance was probably unbearable, as the son who longed to know his maker, while the man himself receded further into books and drink. This man who was once himself bearded and passionate and arrogant. This man who is gone.

•

I have a snapshot of Colin taken a few years ago at Thanksgiving at my mom's house. He's in the kitchen while the cooking is in full flurry, unscrewing a plastic jar of sea salt, listening to 60s on 6 on my stepfather's satellite radio. He's singing along with the song. He looks tender-hearted and as though he's incredibly engaged with this single moment in his life. He looks like he loves and trusts the person holding the camera absolutely. I caught him in an unguarded moment.

•

We all have a sentinel who stands guard, protecting us from pain. Some are more vigilant than others. Depends on how sensitive their protectees are and how much we've been hurt. But they take their jobs very seriously; it's hard to get by them. Music flattens these guys. They go straight to sleep and with them go our defenses.

At first I found it tectonically shocking that Colin's ex had also imagined dancing with him at their wedding to a song from *Moondance*. I am still tempted to be shaken by it. I am tempted to fear that the similarity of her desire invalidates the deep meaning Van has for me, that this thing somehow lessens my partner's love for me. Because she saw the same display I see when he—when *they* sang along with the music. She saw him look down at her all lit up and heartstrong, full of peace and joy.

Or maybe they were frenzied together. Maybe their happiness looked exactly like my lurid obsession. Maybe there was lots of whooping and free-flowing *Aw yeahs* and dancing that didn't need to be broken back down to instinct through years of talk therapy and a painfully slow process of letting go. Maybe my warm-bath happiness actually *doesn't* reach the standard they set. Maybe I'm doing it wrong. Do I listen to the music the same way? Do I do it better? Do I do it worse? Am I missing out on the frenzy I always pictured? Did she understand the frenzy better? Did she live more fully in the frenzy? Was she more fun than I am? Maybe I feel quiet peace in my memory of my happiness because I'm fucking boring as shit.

Or maybe there is a feeling of tremendous relief and accomplishment when you see into a person who is difficult to reach. And maybe music is the best way in. When we're listening to music, singing along, we are our most accessible. We acknowledge and live in our vulnerability when we enjoy music. Music is the corpus callosum of the art forms—it joins the two sides of the brain, allowing intellect to connect with feeling in a process utterly beyond our control.

And we who have listened along with Colin, danced and sung with him, we hold tight to these moments we've seen the light in him turn on;

we are reaching out toward a glimpse of Colin in his purest form—without the controls and stops, with no repression or rationality.

So this girl and I pictured a similar wedding moment. It just means we reached him. At times maybe only for the duration of a song. Four minutes and thirty-four seconds of knowing somebody's insides. Or five minutes and three seconds in which his heart is less blocked, when he seems deeply emotionally available. Two people making a connection conducted by and encased in music. And with Colin, the deepest reach is Van.

Van lets Colin live in gratitude, he teaches him to breathe in beauty. Even the pain is beautiful because it is realized, fully, finally. Van is a gift he treasures so deeply he honors it by sharing it, delivering it proudly into the lives of those he loves. Of course, I wanted to dance at our wedding to "And It Stoned Me." And, naturally, she wanted to see him sing to her: "I long just to hold you tight so I can feel you / Sweet lady of the night." All three of us had carried so much history into this beautiful music.

Van may or may not have known who he was writing about when he wrote songs like "And It Stoned Me" and "Caravan" and "Old Old Woodstock." It doesn't matter. It's clear from how far into our lives his music reaches—he was writing about Colin. And I'm so grateful that he did.

Colin's father may have turned his back on his family, Van may have closed his eyes to the audience, but without the intensity of the love that drove them to recede, where would we be? When I look into Colin as he sings, equal parts peace and torment, off-key and looking down at me, I see the man he might be, the man he often is, I see the man I love to love. And through the prism of his many yesterdays, musical and otherwise, I see that he loves to love me back—today.

Leslie Doyle

Red, Right, Return

"Ants happen."

That was on page three of the six pages of "helpful instructions to get the most out of Beach Glass Cottage." It was between advice for getting the balky lock on the shed door to open and friendly suggestions about where the best fishing sites were. It was too much to read all at one time. I figured I'd consult as necessary.

Ants happen, I thought as I read, but not to me. The first thing I did was head to the nearest Ace for a box of Terro traps. Great stuff. Ecologically sound, too, if you disregard the death of the entire ant colony. Watching the ant train stream back and forth as the members discovered this bonanza and carried their booty to the folks back home gave me pause. I tell myself, it's their choice. They came into my house. But the poison goes back to the whole community.

The next morning, when I can fix breakfast without having to brush an ant off the cutting board every two seconds, I have no more qualms. Death happens, I mutter over the frying pan. I eat my breakfast in antless satisfaction.

"What did you say, Aunt Laurie?" "Nothing, guys—how are your eggs?"

Ants gone, I'm still not alone, of course. The eight and six-year-old boys across the table from me, tearing holes in the middle of their toast to hold up to their faces and stick their tongues through at each other, certainly count as company. I've been counting them plenty, since their mother, my cousin, took off and left them with me. Counting them at the beach, counting them at the supermarket, counting them in the car, just to make sure I didn't lose them along the trip.

"Funny clunking noise from kitchen is icemaker—ignore."

One, two. One, two. One, two. My head echoes like a sound check. One two, one two. Take One. One, two. It's a fucking metronome inside here—the kind of thing I have to remember not to say when I'm with Ricky and Chris. Counting how many days we've been here on this "short vacation, sure, you're mom'll be home really soon—isn't the beach fun?—yeah, I talked to your teachers it's okay." Packets of their schoolwork sit on the kitchen counter, ready to be opened. I couldn't move into their house, which was in foreclosure, and anyway I had no interest in living in the suburban dead zone my cousin, Stacy, had called home. When she showed up last week at my apartment door, kids in tow, I probably didn't ask all the right questions.

Stacy had looked around the place, mentally cataloging, I think, what wasn't there. Television, dishwasher. More than one room. Zack.

She turned to me, and her expression was half, "why am I leaving my kids here," and half, "why am I leaving my kids?" But she said neither. I would have asked her, since it seemed like something I should know, but I didn't want to hurt the boys' feelings.

"This is where you live? You and Zack?" This is where I could have explained how he'd left two nights ago after an amazingly dumb argument, the kind I tell myself not to start. About baseball, if you can believe it. I could have told a pretty good story, made it out so that clearly Zack was at fault. If we weren't talking over the boys' heads. If I'd felt like explaining anything. If Stacy really wanted to know.

"Laurie, I am so embarrassed to ask—it's just for a week or two. Things with Ralph..." She was looking everywhere but at me. This was new for her. "Well, anyway." No, clearly she was not interested in where Zack was. She blinked a few times too many, and her hands shook a little. Which was natural, I guessed under the circumstances. Though I wasn't clear on exactly what the circumstances were.

Chris cried when his mother got back in her car, but Ricky just picked up their backpacks and asked me where to put them.

She'll be back, I told myself, and them, and meanwhile, we all needed to get away. I needed time to work out how to admit I was wrong to Zack, and why I had acted that way. I always liked the shore; I knew the boys would too. So, with Stacy's blessing, we shipped out, down to the cheapest off-season rental I could find.

It's early in the school year. The boys will be fine. I tell myself I will be, too.

"Avoid opening the corner cabinet over the sink all the way. The door has never sat right on its hinges. Just open the left half where the wine glasses are; the rest is empty, anyway."

Thank God for the wine glasses. And the local Acme sells wine.

Putting away the glass from last night, I think of the story Stacy told me the last time we drank together over the phone. The incident she told me about had happened a few years before; Stacy was driving down the highway, late for some kind of meeting, who knows what, something important. Chris was wailing in the back seat, in one of those tub-like baby seats, Ricky all sticky next to him dining on a Cinnabon, spicy sweet goo trickling down his chin. Stacy was steering one handed, the other adjusting the breast pump plugged into the cigarette lighter at one end, and into her at the other, singing along to Paul Simon, "You Can Call Me Al," Ricky singing along with her, all gummed up with Cinnabon cream; Chris just wailing until Stacy found a chance to pull over on the side of the highway and jam the bottle into him.

Or at least that's how I imagined it. My cousin's version was a bit more succinct.

I think I should have listened to it more closely. There was some kind of warning there I missed while we were laughing.

"Open lots of windows to let the house air out. Unlock them first."
I like the smell of damp houses. I know that damp means mildew, damp means unhealthy. But all my life, that grassy wet cardboard smell means vacation to me. A succession of lake cabins, seashore cottages, shacks by rivers; some rented, some borrowed, some visiting friends or friends of friends, all seemed to reek mildly of wet. The rich clamminess signified getting away. We never did Disney vacations or island hops—for me, family trips meant uncomfortably soft mattresses, walls that don't reach the ceiling, other people's food staples pushed to the back of cabinets whose warped doors wouldn't close right, small bookcases jammed with former best sellers and National Geographic, shelves piled with board games in taped together boxes and puzzles of bucolic barns missing three pieces, and mold-stained shower curtains.

I was right at home when I walked in the door the first time. This place had damp to spare. I breathed in deeply.

"If you bring a boat, please follow basic boating rules. Never boat drunk. Watch out for swimmers. Follow red and green channel markers carefully. It's easy to run aground. The way to remember which goes starboard and which goes port depending on whether you're coming or going is—red, right, return. Hope this is clear."
That was Stacy. Breast pumps and Cinnabons. Big house, huge room for each kid. Executive job, executive husband, executive home. Then the job gets downsized, the husband gets lost, the house gets taken back by the bank. They had one of those interest only, adjustable rate mortgages. Balloon tacked on. Well, they hung on for dear life to that balloon, dangling from ropes. Hit the ground pretty hard when the balloon burst. Nothing but empty line in their rope-burned hands, and a whole lot of whose-

fault-is-it. Now Ralph's living in some townhouse rented on money Stacy didn't know he had, and she? I wait for her next call.

"Shed door—key is in drawer to the left of the one under the coffee. Old grayish key. Take care, please—there are no copies."

The night after the ant massacre, I go riding in the dark on a bike I found in the shed behind the cottage, leaving a neighboring teen to babysit the boys. The handlebars are rusted and the gears are a little sticky, but I the tires still have enough air to ride on. There's so much around the place that the owners weren't keeping up with. Maybe someone comes by to ride the bike when no one is renting. This late in the season, that's fairly often, I imagine. Families are all back on school schedules, and everyone else is thinking something else, not the beach. The boys are asleep. I hope. I wonder if their mother is sleeping—or if she's somewhere having fun. I wonder what Zack is doing. I hope he's somewhere not having fun. I pedal harder.

This is the best time down here. There are no crowds. My family came here once in August, and the gridlock was awful. We stayed on the other side of the Canal, in Cape May proper. You'd never know these neighborhoods on the bay side existed, except if you were taking the ferry over to Delaware, and passed them on the road to get there. I bet most vacationers never even see these houses when they pass them. I know I didn't.

From where I'm staying, it's a long bike ride to the ferry park. I wind my way for a couple miles along a road that hugs the edge of the dunes then loops inland for a ways, first to go around a creek inlet, then because of the stretches of bigger houses which push the road, and everyone else, back from the water.

When the road is near the dunes, I can see across the bay to the faint lines of tankers wending their way up the water to Philadelphia. On the main road, I pass some stores. My favorite store sign is the one for "Bargains Galore...And So Much More!" I wonder, as I pass—so, what part isn't the bargains? Everything's lit up by orange street lights; traffic is light. Half the houses are empty now that summer is over.

"The bike doesn't have a headlight."

The time I was here before, Stacy and I were kids, thirteen fourteen; our families came down here together. We were in that obnoxious, nothing is fun stage. We her dad to drop us off at the nearest mall. We were bored right away but wouldn't admit it to each other. We tried to scrape coins out of a fountain when no one was looking, then pretended we'd been throwing them in when someone noticed. We ran up the down escalator—not nearly as fun as it sounds—then she went into the mall version of a head-shop, and came out with her pockets full of patchouli and beads that she hadn't paid for ("Well, it's a hippie shop, right? Freedom and sharing!"). I freaked. She looked at me with pity. "What a dork you are."

She's so right.

Dork enough to share my own life-crisis with her kids while she takes off for wherever.

"When using the bike, stay to the right. I know lots of people here don't. When you run into one going the wrong way, forcing you off the shoulder into the main road, you'll get why it's important not to. Please wear a helmet, too."

I pass a small park, one in the middle of a tidy neighborhood. A sign at the entrance says "Movie Nights in the Park!" I would have thought that they'd be done for the year, but I see that the last date is next Thursday. I make a note to bring the boys; treat them to something fun and different.

The other day we were driving, and I had just been able to catch the alt-rock radio station that broadcasts from part way up the Parkway. You can't hear it up north in North Jersey where I usually live, and you can't usually hear it down here. I was stopped at a red light, on the way home from miniature golf at Sunset Beach, late afternoon, almost dark, the boys clamoring for dinner as we crossed over the canal that connects Cape May City with the rest of New Jersey.

I came to the light, and for once, the station came in clearly. The summer season over, I was the only car on the road. The song playing caught me ear, and I stayed there, through the red, through the green, through another red. Chris and Ricky started getting restless in the back seat. It took a minute, but they finally figured out that they were hungry, and not moving.

That time Stacy told me about the breast pump and the cigarette lighter, she paused, like I was a tad slow, when I asked why she didn't just stop the car and nurse Chris. "Right. And how was I going to get anywhere that way?"

There at the light, the singer was saying, "Cause in my head there's a Greyhound station/Where I send my thoughts to far off destinations." I felt a need to keep listening, to know what he was talking about. There was a pause after "Greyhound" and at first I thought, there's a dog in his head. Odd. Chris kicked my seat, bringing me back to the car. "Aunt Laurrieee," Ricky droned in an exaggerated whine only an eight-year-old can produce.

"We're hungry." I switched off the station. We drove home, stopping at Rainbow Palace for ice cream. I'm not sure Stacy would approve, but she's not here, is she?

So, Movie Night at the Park. Might be another distraction.

Finally, I reach the ferry terminal, my legs aching from the unaccustomed exercise of pedaling. It's late. A ferry is turning into the canal between the jetties that reach out into the Bay. It must be the last one of the night. It's lit up like a Mississippi River paddleboat, but glides by almost silently, passing first between the channel markers at the ends of the jetties—green on the one closest to me, red across the canal.

The movie will actually be a couple of short sci-fi B movies from the fifties. It's billed as "Back Again to the Future." Hope the boys will like this. They don't see much black and white. If Zack were here, we'd play "Mystery Science Theater 3000."

My phone hasn't rung at all. But I've had some time to do some thinking. I'm feeling like a pretty bad aunt right now, leaving the boys asleep with an almost stranger in the house. I didn't tell them before I left, because they're already feeling insecure. I needed to get out, just for an hour. The babysitter, Kara, is the merry cheerleader type; she said she wasn't worried about them waking up to find her there instead of me. They've said hi to her as we come and go the past few days, so it's not like she's a complete stranger, I tell myself.

It's weird how vacation houses are all mixed in with the homes of the locals down here. Kara's family rents the cottage next door. I don't see her parents much. Her dad works fishing boats, mom waitresses sporadically. Kara's hoping to go to the local CC next year for a respiratory therapy certification, if she can afford a car and insurance to get there. It took about five minutes of knowing her to learn all this. She's happy to let me overpay her for this last minute job. When I get back to the house, she curled up in the least lumpy living room chair, working on homework.

"The boys never woke up," she tells me. Kara takes my overly large guilt tip with palpable glee, and heads off to add it to her car fund. I look at her and wonder how I so quickly went from being her to being me—it seems like just last week that Stacy and I were going up that escalator, illicit pennies in our pockets.

"The telephone is local only. You can take other calls but you can't call out. Sort of Hotel California-ish, in a way."

I'm beginning to have serious questions about the owners of this house. I make a note to ask Kara about them the next time I see her.

So yeah. The argument with Zack? Like I said, it was about baseball, which I take ridiculously seriously. Zack does, too, in an adult kind of way, as opposed to my pre-adolescent blind adoration of the team. So when he stated, over a beer, while watching our team again losing in its familiar September swoon kind of way, that really, "ya gotta admit" that the third baseman of the rival team that was currently beating us might actually be better than our star third baseman, I took it personally.

I realize that doesn't say much good about me. I managed to take this mild comment and blow it into a dispute about loyalty and faithfulness, and wow, a lot of stuff that left Zack blinking at first, then kind of clamming up, and then finally storming out—in his quiet Zack kind of way, back to the apartment he nominally still shared with a couple roommates, though his clothes were mostly all here at my place.

This has gone on far too long. So I call him. And admit that saying Ryan Zimmerman is better than David Wright probably doesn't mean that Zack has commitment issues. And he's apparently glad enough to hear from me that he doesn't pursue the topic of why I went there. And I ask him, if he's still talking to me, to come down to the shore, since I'm still dealing with the boys. We agree that I will stay down here for another week or until one of their parents comes to his or her senses, and Zack will try to stop down in a few days.

Then I decide it's time to call Stacy.

We had talked once since I got here; she'd called me a few days ago. She gave me a "new number" but asked me not to call unless it was an emergency.

She had left me in charge of her two young sons; I said I thought it was important to know what she considered an emergency. She waited a couple beats before answering.

"You'll know." So it's up to me, right? And I say it's an emergency. The emergency is—she needs to get her ass over here and see her kids. I'm plying them with miniature golf and ice cream and movies in the park. Clearly they need a real adult—not me, not Kara. Not even Zack, who will be great fun when he gets here, but is in no way a parent stand-in.

The number rings a long time. I'm about to give up when a voice I don't recognize answers in a bored tone.

"Horizons Rehabilitation."

"You'll note the pot and towel on living room floor. Please empty any accumulated water and put them back before you leave; positioned under the ceiling light near the wicker rocker. If there's a strong wind and the ceiling leaks, no worries—just get the pot to catch the water."

We spend the next couple days mucking along the tidal flats. Some communities along the bay have a "beach." We have mud. Acres of it.

Miles of it. It feels like you could walk all the way to Delaware some days at low tide. Ricky and Chris collect molted horseshoe crab shells which congregate in little piles of translucent casings on the back step. There are so many they crackle under our feet. Sometimes the boys bring home whole dead ones, the really big ones. I make them keep them outside; they start to stink pretty quickly.

I tell them that they should never, ever, hurt a live one. Lots of people do, because they think they are dangerous, but they are not. Or maybe, I guess, they just think it's funny. To tell you the truth, I don't know why some people do what they do. I tell the boys that the horseshoe crabs have copper-based blood that turns a beautiful turquoise blue when they bleed, and I can see them looking at the rotting mud-brown carcasses and not believing me. I tell them, also, that this blood is used by medical companies to make sure that stuff like intravenous drugs and medical devices are bacteria-free. Most crabs survive the procedure to remove some blood, but a few do not. Of course, using their blood that way makes no difference to the horseshoe crabs. Dead is dead, as far as they are concerned. I don't say this last part to the boys.

They figure I am making this stuff up. But it's all true; I saw a documentary on them once. It interested me because my grandmother was dying of cancer at the time, which was right after I graduated college. I was taking care of her; my parents were not to be around much. Actually, they were hardly ever around. All those family vacations? They were me tagging along with my aunt and uncle and cousins, including Stacy. This grandmother, the one who was dying, was my mom's mother, the other side of the family, so it was up to me to move into her house and wash her and get her to the bathroom. And watch her die. There were a lot of tubes and ports and stuff all around the room, attached to her in too many places. I wondered if there was a way to figure out if the horseshoe crab blood had been used on them, maybe some streaks of blue on the tubes, but I couldn't find any.

There is a Greyhound station in Stacy's head. Or maybe a greyhound. Something is tearing her brain apart with yellow fangs. Or maybe she's the greyhound in her own head, running around a track after a fake rabbit. If that's what greyhounds really do. I don't know; I've only seen cartoons.

It took a while to get the rehab folks to put Stacy on the phone. She's still in the detoxing phase of her program, getting off the smorgasbord of pills she'd been chewing while things were falling apart, and I have to convince them that I'm an emergency.

When she comes to the phone, finally, she tells me she's figured out a way to get Ralph's insurance to pay; I hope she's right, even though that wasn't the question I was asking. She also tells me she can't cope now, she's sorry, really sorry, but Ralph will get the boys next week. It turns out he didn't know where she'd stashed them. He'll be down just as soon as he can get a day off from his new job.

I take the boys to the park by the ferry one afternoon. The people on the ferry cling to the railings with one hand, while waving at everyone at the dock like they're taking off for a trans-Atlantic voyage. It's a windy day. I have to be careful that neither boy blows off the rocks when we walk out to the end of the jetty. They have always lived on flat ground, with sidewalks and buses to school. They aren't very sure-footed.

"Sand happens, too. Sweep before you go, but don't worry if you don't get every grain. We never do."

The night before Zack is due to get here, I go for my last late night bike ride. Kara is thrilled to be overpaid by me again. It's a particularly dark night. On some side streets with no streetlights or occupied houses, it's so dim I can't see the road. I steer by guessing. I hope any passing cars will see me.

Before I go, I ask Kara about the owners of my cottage. She says they didn't used to rent it out. They lived there full time, them and their son Tyler. No, she didn't know him that well; he was a few years older. Haven't seen them much since he came back from Iraq. Nice people, always a little odd in an ordinary kind of way, but nice. Didn't own a car, biked everywhere. It turns out that I am blowing my meager savings on an unplanned vacation from my highly contingent career plan as a telemarketer, and they are using my rent to pay for the hotel room next to the VA, where Tyler is rehabilitating.

Coming back up the road along the dunes, I overtake another woman out riding. She's has a determined, biker-person look about her, but I'm going faster and I'm pretty smug as I catch up to pass. The reflector on the back of her bike glints red in the lights from the ferry terminal over the dunes to our right. I swing wide to the left pedaling hard to go by. But then I think—maybe she's ill, maybe she's on chemo—who knows what's slowing her down. And I stop feeling so smug.

"When you leave: Be careful to close up all the windows. Rain gets in easily. Drive by the water one last time on your way out. Especially if it's late. The sunsets are always worth seeing. We haven't caught a green flash yet, but we look every time. Let us know if you see one."

The next evening is "Movie Night in the Park." Zack shows up around noon. He's ordered tickets for the next Mets/Nats game. I think he's almost afraid to tell me in case I think he's prolonging the argument, but I can tell a reconciliation motion when I see one. After a while, I send him out the door with the boys, and they've been fishing all day. They come home with some spotted hake, and I fry them up for dinner. Zack tells me that there were lots of these to catch because the flesh is so fragile that the commercial fishermen don't bother with it. Chris and Ricky make faces, then eat it all.

At the park that evening, it's cold. We bundle up, but it's not enough to keep the late September air from creeping through every layer. The boys are bored by the black and white movies at first—where we see retro rocket ship funkiness, they see bad production values.

Chris eventually falls asleep on my lap. I'm suggesting we go, but Ricky's gotten engrossed in the story, after all. Or maybe in the projector, the beam of light trailing through the soft night air before landing on the side of the field house which is being used as a screen. I tell him his brother is cold and tired, and they both had a long day outside. But Ricky is having none of it.

He starts to run, away from us and up toward the screen. On it, a rocket that looks like something out of the Jetsons is taking off into space, and the screen fills with a scene of twinkling stars against the darkness of the universe, crumbling at the corners where the cinder block walls of the building have cracked. Standing up there, he catches the rays of the movie, causing a big, Ricky-shaped shadow to fall across the picture, which leads to a lot of shouting and trouble. I am still holding Chris, so Zack runs up to grab Ricky, who is oblivious to all the commotion he is causing. He is looking down at his body, covered with stars, a boy-sized constellation across his chest and arms, and in his hair. He is beaming at his hands when Zack plucks him from in front of the screen.

He doesn't want to leave. We tell him that the movie is almost over. We tell him not to listen to the mean stuff people are saying about his behavior. We tell him that everything's going to be alright. That he'll be going home soon.

We tell him all sorts of stuff. Some of it is true. By the time we get home, both he and his brother are asleep in the car, and we carry them into the house, the discarded shells of the horseshoe crabs crackling under our feet.

Natasha Murdock

The Curve of My Neck

Maybe you'd say it's like a Stradivarius. My fingers
sliding through Adagio for Strings softly,
each wisp rising to sound.
You'd like to teach me,
placing your hands over my mine to play.
Slowly overtaking the crescendo,
while the violin turns into the crease
of my thigh, and my hands change into
lips, all over the backs of your arms
and palms.

And then we're a tangle
    of limbs and specificities and strings and urgencies and fingertips
forgetting
the rest of the composition and coming
to rest ourselves on the hard,
hard earth of the desert.

Or maybe, you'd say, it's like a neck,
just a neck like any other, and leave it.

Joseph Mills

Death And My Daughter: A Timeline

When she is three,
we drive back roads,
passing burial grounds,
and each time she sees one,
she yells with a delight
similar to finding Easter eggs,
Look! More dead people!

When she is four,
coming home from daycare,
she suddenly says,
Daddy, when I'm dead,
please don't leave me outside
in the rain to get wet.
Please bring me inside. Please.

At five, she tells her grandmother,
I know what happens when you die
you either get boxed up or cooked.

At six, she tells me
as I work on the roof,
Don't worry, Daddy, I'm here.
If you fall and break your legs,
I'll go get Maman. If you fall
and die, I'll call 9-1-1-1-1.
Don't worry, I'm right here.

And when the neighbor dies
and her kindergarten classmate dies,
and her friend's baby brother dies,
what upsets her is the silence
that follows. After the memorials
no one mentions them anymore.
No one speaks their names.
It's like they've just disappeared,
so when she is seven, she says,
Please talk about me after I'm dead,
and when we tell her we hope
to die first she becomes concerned.
But, I'd be lonely without you.
Maybe, we can all die together
and that way we can stay together.
I want us to stay together, she says,
But, we'll need a pretty big box.

M.C. Mah
2014 Earl Weaver Baseball Writing Prize Finalist

Top 10 Oakland A's Prospects[1]

1. Addison Russell, SS. In the throes of the internet, it's that time of year when we can hardly wait for someone else to put the Oakland Athletics' Top 10 prospects in proper order. The top of the list is a no-brainer. Tools, skills, young for his league, and he's going to stick at short. I have never seen motion video of an infielder approximating what I believe Addison Russell to look like, but I have to say I've never seen anything like him in the green and gold since Eric Chavez or Miguel Tejada.

Update: On July 4th, the Cubs acquired Addison Russell and Billy McKinney (spoiler alert: #3 on this list) for pitchers Jeff Samardzija and Jason Hammel. A risky trade; your author got word late that night and acted as if a child had been ripped from his arms.

2. Daniel Robertson, SS/3B. It is a wonder just how much has been made free. But in a democracy of information, expertise becomes subjective. This is only natural and disastrous. Not to mention circular. Rather often the true concern of such expertise (i.e., on the Oakland farm system) is revealed to be but excess aplomb with the internet itself. The effect can be overstated, but I really do think we care about what other people think more than any human population ever has. Someone out there thinks Daniel Robertson has a short swing. It's a fact that many assume he'll have to move to third. So he must have the arm.

3. Billy McKinney is an outfielder drafted out of high school in Texas. He hit 326/387/437 in his first 55 professional games. You could have looked that up anywhere. It's freely available information. If we can no longer have expertise, the best we can hope for, oddly enough, is authority.

4. Bobby Wahl, RHP. You don't have to measure your life the way a baseball player does his career, but just in case you want to: you'd rather be an exceptional talent as early as high school. There's nothing wrong with college, but, preferably, you should find no compelling reason to go. You want to debut by 22 or 23. You want to know what you're doing by then, because the average age of one's finest year is a quick turnaround: 27. Where your physical peak meets the learning curve. After that, you want to get by on experience, cultivated skills: power, discipline, savvy. At 35, even a natural could be done, and we haven't discussed what your ultimate upside (*ceiling*, the ideal best you could have done with yourself) was in the first place. Bobby Wahl is 21.2 innings out of college. He could be anything. I could have been anything. But turns out that, at his age, I was already most of what I turned out to be. Maybe Bobby Wahl is the same, and he struck out 11.6/9 in a small sample.

5. Raul Alcantara, RHP. What do you do with your brain? There's room in my brain for Raul Alcantara's miniscule walk rate. But what do you do with the rest if you're not inclined to set more and more of it aside for baseball? Do you have to think about the nature of art that entire time? Do you have to stifle lusts that would otherwise swallow your life whole? What about consider your responsibilities to others? Deprived of being able to simply care about who wins, do you have to think about what right you have to think what you think? What constant panic! Bless you.

6. Billy Burns, OF. Fast, and a potential WAR monster in center if defensive metrics are to be believed. Baseball is a set of information. It's vast, but subject to mastery in a way that other passions are not. The information is discrete: the names of the players, numbers. There are game concepts but no moral questions. To establish fluency in other spheres means that you have to defend what you know about data-mining, or the Middle East. You have to question the tactical aggression of the Democratic Party. You have to be out of your depths. Not that sports is without unfounded opinion. Just the opposite. It's more like everyone involved understands how little their opinion matters. Sports chat is purer for it. We all know where the field is. There are lines which, if close to being crossed, kick up a cloud of chalk.

7. Nolan Sanburn, RHP. So goes the prevailing rhetoric that if I part with consensus at any point, I'll be overrating, or underrating, a prospect. I think we can enrich our spirit, and our language, if we never use these hurtful terms again. It might be strange to see Nolan Sanburn here—I don't know if he has two pitches, much less the three he needs to start—but his floor is providing high-leverage relief innings, while Matt Olson and Renato Nunez, with those kind of ratios, will become data points about the importance of discipline, even in youth.

8. Michael Ynoa, RHP. Last splash in the unregulated Dominican market, arm trouble, "beautiful eyes," according to Santiago Casilla.In the event that you do not watch a game at seven, and another on the west coast at ten, your evening is spent taking in some other part of our culture; the internet, literature, a movie, golden-age TV. And you wake up in the morning, freshly recapped, to find yourself, according to many critics, a philistine and a racist. How dare you, sir.

9. B.J. Boyd, OF. In a sense, the culture has caught up with sports fandom. It seems it has gotten more difficult to explain or justify what one does with their time. As a reflex, we disclaim our need to watch, to validate, to know, as irrational. We feel the lowered bar of our obsessions. But I think we're channeling a drive which has been for so many of us ably sated by picking which ball they like to see in the air, supporting the franchise nearest their hometown, and relenting to a particular vulnerability, one which savors small victories and shakes off inevitable losses. I really think the rest of you are on the boards at Reddit, wrongfully accusing someone of murder. Just watch the game.

10. Chris Kohler, LHP. Follow something. Let it operate without your contribution. Reacquaint yourself with caring about that which has nothing to do with you. Can you believe it? At some point, this was recognizably human behavior. And then I had to go and rank Kohler, from baseball hotbed and confirmed real place Rancho Cucamonga, tenth among Oakland Athletics prospects.

---

[1]Originally published by *Cobalt Review* on July 16, 2014.

Ryan W. Bradley

This Dirty, Self-Cleaning Universe

After Ruth Stone

Every time I thought I was dead I was at peace,
especially when the tumor showed up over night,
big as a softball and attached like an anemone
to a muscle above my shoulder blade
and when it was cut out of me the surgeon
looked like the definition of panic, still there was
this calm. The same calm as when my wife
was in labor with our son and the doctor
was off delivering someone else's baby
and it was so real that my wife and I might
have to bring our son into the world ourselves,
just as we had made him. At that moment I thought,
I've got this. And then the doctor showed up
and delivered him while I held my wife's hand,
repeating the same assurance over and over.
And then the surgeon came into the room
and told me the tumor was benign and even she
looked surprised and I was left feeling empty
of all my preparation. Yes, it's a dirty world,
a universe off all the wrong expectations,
all the wrong results. Somehow, though,
the pieces always seem to know how to fit
as if the puzzle was made by design,
which is how you know the universe is not a poet.

Wes Civilz
2014 Frank McCourt Creative Nonfiction Prize Finalist

excerpt from *Action: A Memoir Of Lust*

After we have sex I drive Kelly home, and on the way back I feel happy and sad. There's always that tinge of emptiness, after.

My dash clock says 12:03 a.m., and I pull into the twenty-four-hour Safeway for some groceries. I feel strange, off-balance somehow, moving through these aisles…I think I've gone too quickly from fucking mode to feeding mode. The cantaloupes look like boobs. All the foods have sex meanings: bananas, cream, eggs. Look at the names of these cuts of meat: breasts, thighs, rump roast.

I pass by boxes of microwave stuffing. Even plain old stuffing makes me think of stuffing a woman. What am I, twelve?

Shaving a pussy is something I haven't done for a while, I realize, as I look down the aisle with razors and shaving cream. I could really go to do that again. Kelly has a little grown in right now, which I like, but maybe she'll let me shave her the next time she comes by. When I pass by a college girl in the frozen goods aisle, I think: *Tonight I am satisfied, so I don't need to obsessively fantasize about sleeping with you.* But a little part of me wants her even more than normal *because* I just got laid. I want to fuck and fuck and fuck. I want to die fucking, heart attack during orgasm.

I inspect the women's magazines in the checkout aisle: *30 Ways to Seduce a Man Without Trying.*

20 Sex Moves that Will Make Him a You-Junkie.

The 10 Worst Ways to Say Yes.

Do Your Walk of Shame with Pride, Girl!

I see how these magazines create the anxiety that they attempt to soothe. A brilliant business model, really—be both the problem and the solution. Like how if you use antacids too much, your heartburn will get worse. When I buy one of the mags, the checkout guy snorts and looks at me funny. I don't like being looked at funny, normally, but when I have pussy juice dried on my thighs, nothing can shake me. This is my magazine, dude, and I'm going to read it carefully. I'm going to learn how the other side thinks.

•

From an article called "Cougar Techniques:"

Unleash your inner cougar! Don't sit at home wondering about younger men—these days, more and more boys are the May in May-December romances. What he lacks in experience, he'll more than make up for with his youthful stamina...

A few days later, breasts are in my hands—not Kelly's. These belong to a woman I met at a bar downtown called Plush. We had a lot of vodka-sodas and came back to my place, and I think her boobs may be the softest things I've ever touched. She self-identifies as a cougar...she seems to think I'm quite a bit younger than I am...she tells me she's in her forties, but she has the absurdly youthful breasts of an eighteen-year-old. I caress them over and over, mesmerized.

We don't hook up again. I send her the *sorry-but-I'm-disappearing* text. Of course I put it in nicer words than that. Cougar or not, I fear that because she is in her forties, she is looking for something serious only.

I don't do serious.

I see her in the bars a couple of times after this. One time I'm pretty buzzed, and I go over and talk to her, even though I feel embarrassed. She keeps calling me Houdini. "He was the master of disappearing," she says.

"I thought he was the master of escaping," I say.

"Hmm," she says.

She will not go home with me again. I go to bed very late and drunk and alone.

•

When I wake up the next day, the clock on my bedside table is being a jerk. It's looking at me funny. It seems to be saying: *it's two in the afternoon, you lazy piece of shit—how's that hangover going?*

"I don't have a hangover," I say. Well, okay, I do have one...but it's the workable kind. I may be a little woozy, and have some heartburn going, and I may have a little bit of that feeling again. That feeling of hating myself. But it's workable.

I have to get rid of this clock. My friends and I have a tradition of giving each other tasteless, god-awful gifts. It's an art, finding something that people will truly hate, and last Christmas I was presented with this horror...a pink, sparkly, Hello Kitty alarm clock. It has a digital cat face, female I assume, that meows and grins and murmurs stuff in Japanese. Her green eyes blink with a thoroughly unsettling cuteness. This cat lays a lot of bullshit on me in that weird hallucination zone between sleeping and waking. I can't seem to throw her away, though.

I shower and eat both Pop-Tarts from my last two-pack. I drink coffee and head out to a bar pretty close by, the Shelter, and there is this girl playing pool there, and oops, back to my place we go, and we lie down on my bed and make out, and I take out her breasts and *good lord*. She's kind of chubby, and her plumpness has resulted in a pair of giant, stout, impossible boobs, and they have proud pointy bullet-nipples that make me feel like babies are being denied something rightfully theirs. I know it's rude to stare, but Jesus...

She pulls them out of my hands and covers up with a sheet. "I feel objectified," she says. She's smiling, though.

We never see each other again. The next day, I send out the sorry-but-I-must-disappear text.

"??" she texts back. "I don't get it. ☹"

Not even the epic boobs are enough to make me stay. I'm already running away. Once I've started running, I can't stop.

•

I will never be satisfied. I know this. There is never enough, and I can see there's something grim and mirthless in my quest. Ass, ass, ass. One ass makes me crave another ass, which makes me crave yet another ass. If there is a small ass, I want a big ass; if I get a big ass, I want a small one again. I want a girl who isn't white then I want a white girl. I want, I want, I want…I am a bottomless vortex of wanting.

I need to pick up a few things at the drug store. As I park I remember a cute girl that works the cash here sometimes. Strawberry-blonde hair, perfect little hands. Maybe she'll be working today. I walk in, and yes, she's here. God, if she looks this good in an ill-fitting Walgreen's uniform, imagine what she's like in a dress. I realize I can get only three of the five things I came for (toothpaste, floss, Ibuprofen) because I can't bring myself to put toilet paper and condoms down on the counter in front of this girl, I just can't. She doesn't say much as she rings me up, but I get a smile at the end, and I give her one back, and I want to tease her in some way, but I chicken out and leave. I drive to Target for the TP and condoms.

Target: theoretically, the store is a giant room with shelves of stuff you might want, the aisles being a sort of negative space that allows you to look over the stuff. The problem, the paradox, is that Target's aisles are filled with women, and they are also something I want. There's so many I can hardly shop. I find myself wandering down aisles with things I don't need, like pet stuff (I have no pets) just to walk by certain beauties. They must know I'm creeping on them. Look at this one. I quickly scan butt, waist, shoulders, hair, cute little hat, please turn around, yes, boobs…oh, boobs so snug in that sweater. Why won't you just jump into my big red cart? I would roll you out to my car and bring you home to a new life of luxury and leisure. And lick your pussy every night.

I go to a male cashier for my condoms and toilet paper. I can't face a woman with them. He runs the box of rubbers under the scanner, and smiles. "Ultra-thins," he says. "These things are the best."

"Totally, bro," I say. *Don't talk to me.*

I head to my favorite bar for happy hour, and the waitresses there drive me crazy. I'm crazy, they're crazy, their power over me is crazy. I get things done on my laptop, I respond to emails, I grade papers…but I am, make no mistake about it, going slowly crazy. There's a boner chafing against my jeans.

I'm going to turn thirty-five soon…and I still feel like I'm going to be called up to the chalkboard in middle school.

•

From the short article, "Bottoms Up!:"

> *Toting a little extra in the derrière department? A new study shows that 76 percent of men aged 18 to 80 prefer a rear end in the "large" or "very large" categories!*

The internet coughs up a girl. I'm not going to tell you what site I met her on, because it embarrasses me. She is a pleasant but excruciatingly normal young woman. Nowhere near weird enough for me.

But…her butt.

She has this giant, yet shapely—this massive, yet well-proportioned—booty. From the moment I see it, I'm a goner. I have to release this ass. I must free it from her skirt and hold the thing in my hands. We're in my living room, and she keeps getting up and walking around as she talks, and her ass is shifting back and forth so pleasingly with that mystical side-to-side rhythm that will fascinate us boys to the end of time.

Now we're lying on my bed. I'm giving her a massage, and I pull down the zipper on her skirt. She giggles but does not resist, and now I can see a few inches of crack. I pull the skirt down, and her underwear too, and now the great pale ass is before me. Like two outsized soufflés sitting next to each other on a kitchen counter. I kiss her butt all over. Surprising myself, I stick my tongue down into the crack. I've never rimmed a girl before. It feels really naughty, and I do it for a while. She keeps arching her back, and pushing her butt back into my face. I could suffocate under her butt and die happy.

She pulls her skirt back up, and says that we can't keep doing this—

there's something wrong about it.

"Is there?" I say.

We look at each other.

"You're crazy," she says. She's blushing. "I mean, we can't kiss now... after you've done *that*."

"I guess not."

We walk to my front door. We hug awkwardly. We never see each other again.

•

When I knock, he answers the door Corona in hand. This is my neighbor, a crazy motherfucker named Pluto, and we're going to hit the town tonight and procure some fillies. Pluto's a cowboy-hat-wearing chef with a chronic pussy habit; over the past few years he's become my main wingman. Tonight he's got a white cowboy hat on, a leather jacket, and alligator skin boots. "Got my gators on, bitch," he says, "somebody stop me. All right, let's watch a scene."

He slides in the DVD: *Pimps of America*. We've been watching this documentary a little too much. It's like a locker-room ritual before we head out to the bars.

This pimp is sitting in a barber's chair, on his cell phone, discussing business with one of his girls. He calls her bitch in the same tone a regular guy might call his girlfriend honey. "Listen, bitch—all you gotta do is get me my money, bitch, and we good. Just handle my bidness and we right as rain, bitch." His tone sounds almost...affectionate. "Errythang gonna be all right, bitch. Holla atcha lata, bitch."

Pimping isn't all beating up your stable of whores and injecting them with drugs against their will.

When we get to Hotel Congress, the women drive us crazy. What is a man to do with all these females? A girl walks by with this ass. It is, like, *the* ass. It might be described as a shelf. It is not large, but it juts out from her back like a hump from a camel. You could set a drink on top of this thing, and that drink would not spill. "Are you kidding me?" Pluto says, rubbernecking, "Are you fucking kidding me?"

We circle around for a better view. Ass, ass, ass, my brain whispers, like a sample looping through a DJ's set.

But I'm afraid. I've never fully conquered my fear of talking to women. The terror. The verbal blunders. The heart rate jacking up. The best I can do is to sometimes trick myself into it. What you have to do is start talking before you think about what to say. If you're standing there pre-choosing words, you've already lost the battle. Like the drill sergeant yelled to his cadets in this Special Forces training movie I saw: *don't think, just do!*

•

Sometimes they talk to you, though. It can happen. Two butch girls (lip-rings, short hair) come over to us. *Are you guys gay, are you guys gay?* They need an answer, stat.

No, I say, *are you girls gay?*

No, we're roommates.

They're totally gay. Which is fine, but then why do they seem to be flirting with us?

Oh: they are using us as male pawns in a game of lesbian jealousy chess. Interesting.

The one that starts flirting with me says her name is Andie. *With an* i *and an* e, she says, and I think, *Here we go.*

After a while, the one who's flirting with Pluto, Rosie, comes over and slaps me. Hard.

I say, *That kind of turns me on.*

Rosie says, *Why am I not surprised you like that shit…*

Twenty minutes and a round of shots later, she's punching the air near Andie's head. She's pretty angry now. She comes back my way and punches in front of my nose. I can feel the air shudder. She punches again and actually connects, but just a little bit, a kiss, not enough to hurt. I rub my nose and she stomps off to the bathroom.

Andie sits down next to me with a fresh drink, saying, *Rosie has major issues about men.* Andie really wants me to go to another bar with her. *Pleeeeeeeease*, she says.

Is it worth making Rosie this jealous? I ask.

Don't make me beg, she says.

Actually, begging might work, I say. *Begging turns me on.*

She gets down on her knees and pushes in between my legs, laying a cheek on my thigh and looking up at me. I realize she has a serious submissive side, like so many pushy people do.

Puh-leeeeeeeeese come to another bar with me, she says.

If you beg some more, I say, *then maybe.* She is not beautiful but she has really big eyes and I like looking into them as she stares up at me and implores. Watery female saucers of pleading. I'm getting kind of hard. My half-boner is really close to her cheek and I wonder if she's noticed it. *It totally turns you on to beg*, I say.

Like it's not turning you on, too, you fucking pervert, she says. She rubs her cheek gently against my thigh, and it brushes my dick, and I realize that she is just as dirty as me, and that she has some seriously unresolved feelings for boys, and I feel bad for these two girls because they clearly have a rocky road ahead. Also I wish Andie would blow me right now, her kneeling just like this. I wish the rest of the bar would vanish in a puff of smoke and she'd unzip my jeans and commence. I agree to go to another bar, and the four of us leave, Rosie walking ahead with Pluto. Andie tells me how at her house she has a sex dungeon; that I should check it out sometime. She says: *Latex, whips, gags—the works.*

Hmm. It might be worth staying in touch with these highly strung scissor-sisters.

I consider Andie's fairly monumental ass, how it could probably take quite a spanking. Yes, that butt could be slapped with great zest and concentration in some dank dungeon, and a good time would be had by all.

But of course we're never going to see each other again.

Rosie is piggybacking on Pluto. They careen down Congress Street, both of them way too drunk for it. Pluto jumps off a curb and when they land, Rosie bites her tongue on his head—I hear the resounding bonk of her jaw on his skull. She dismounts and walks in silence, hand over her mouth. There's a little blood.

When we get to the bar Andie and I head back to the bathrooms and Rosie watches us go with jealous eyes, but does not follow. The men's room is occupied, but there is no one in the women's. I pull Andie inside and lock the door, and we look into each other's eyes, and we share a deep feeling of resignation like, *how many times have I meaninglessly kissed a stranger before?* and we start making out. We keep at it, even though it's all dead lips. I grip her ass and mash my hands over her breasts. After all, her body is here and I know she will let me. More than wanting to feel her body, I want to feel her letting me grab anywhere I want.

I notice that her shoulder has popped out of her shirt, and it looks good, so I give it a little chomp. She doesn't flinch. I bite harder and still no flinch. I say, *Wow, it takes a lot to hurt you. Damn right,* she says. On the same arm, she shows me the marks where she has cut herself.

Tiny razor slashes, many of them, in a row. Most have healed, except the last few.

Andie has a huge grin now and a fierce pride in her eyes.

I feel empathy and I stop manhandling her. I reach out and gently touch her scars, sliding the ridges under my fingers. They have a creepy beauty. Pain's gorgeousness. She lets me touch and starts unbuttoning her jeans. *You've got to check out my thigh, it's crazy...*

There are more slashes down there, bigger, nastier ones, leading all the way down to the knee, and I kneel down to inspect them, but suddenly the bathroom door goes *BANG! BANG! BANG!* The thing is nearly coming off its hinges. I unlock it and it's Rosie, of course. Pluto is standing behind her, with a look that says, *Here we go...*

Rosie screams, top of her lungs: *ANDIE, WHAT THE FUCK ARE YOU DOING IN HERE?*

Then she says, in this quiet, freaky voice, *Let's go find guys somewhere else, honey.*

A bouncer appears. He's angry. *You*, he says, pointing at me, *need to get them*, pointing at the girls, *the fuck out of here!*

Which seems to me like he's passing the buck on his own responsibilities...but I try an exploratory pull on Andie's shoulders. She resists like a mule, her face reddening. She's coming up with something really nasty to say to Rosie, I can see it bubbling up behind her eyes. Pluto and I walk out of the bar and relegate the situation to memory.

•

When my alarm goes off the next morning, the cat face blinks on and she immediately starts in with some bullshit. "Hasn't something gotten lost?" she says.

"Huhmmnn?" I can only get one eye open.

"Hasn't something gotten lost along the way?" she says, scrunching up her little whiskered nose.

I smack the snooze button, located between the molded plastic ears.

•

From an article called "Telling Him What He Needs to Be Told:"

> *Men are simple creatures—they respond well when given clear instructions. Learn to make your ideas understood in one clear, simple thought, as opposed to hinting and/or expecting him to read your signals...*

I sleep with Kelly again. A long, rough, exhausting, awesome fuck. The kind that makes you feel like a plaque should be mounted on the bedroom door when you're done. She leaves nail marks on my back, and I smile with pride when I notice them in the bathroom mirror. We go out for drinks afterward, and as she's ordering a glass of wine I see that her neck is still flushed. A flushed neck on a woman is one of the great things.

Kelly says, "What did you do last weekend?" and gives me a look. The female look that means this isn't small talk.

"Some girl invited me to her sex dungeon," I say, "but I didn't end up going."

"Shut up," she says, smirking.

"Her lesbian lover got too jealous."

"Shut *up*. You're never serious."

I shut up, and so does she for a while. She's thinking. I'm figuring that she's going to force me to talk about what really happened over the weekend, but instead she says, "I can't marry you."

"What?" I say. "I don't remember proposing."

She carefully sips her wine. "What I mean is, I can't fall in love with you. I'm going to be thirty in two years. If we keep sleeping together like this, I'm going to fall in love with you."

"Okay…"

"Clearly you aren't interested in being a father. Or a husband. Or even in falling in love."

"I don't know what to say."

•

We saw each other a few more times. Then one day she flew to the Bay Area. And suddenly made babies with a bland somebody. I gather from the internet that the guy has a high-paying job of some sort, or is possibly independently wealthy. The facts aren't that clear. Goodbye, Kelly.

Olvard Liche Smith

Grand Gesture

We've been perched on the telephone wires all day, bearing gifts. There are many of us, more of us than you can count, each beak holding a special something. One of us holds a Simply Lemonade bottle-cap because that's Girlfriend's favorite drink. Another holds a discarded Wendy's wrapper that he said came from an Asiago Chicken Sandwich, because Girlfriend can't get enough of them, she swears they put crack in it. Many others are holding fortunes from those Chinese cookies, or assorted clips, pins, and other shiny things. I, myself, am holding a live salamander. It's squirming and I feel sorry for it, especially because the other pigeons think I'm strange and stubborn, that the salamander suffers for no good reason, but I am their leader and that means respect, which means they don't fight me on the things I consider important. *This reptile will be the vessel for my feelings and that's that*, I told them this morning as we landed on the wires. *Trust me, I know these things.* And they do trust me; that's something I appreciate. So we've remained perched all day in the August swelter, with our breasts thrust forward as if we were robins and not pigeons, silent and imperial. Girlfriend's out, but she will be back soon. We watch and wait.

A red Mustang flies into the neighborhood, disregarding the stop sign, and brakes on a dime. We know who the car belongs to and we're immediately compelled to crap on the windshield. I catch one of us hunching forward, prepping for flight. *Wait*, says my gesture, a single raised wing, *let's just see what he does.*

Boyfriend remains stopped in front of Girlfriend's house, right in the middle of the street. He doesn't even bother flashing the hazards, he just puts it in park, sits there daring the traffic with a mean expression, a face that says *do somethin' nigga*. Cars whip around him violently, grazing the front bumper of the Nissan heading the opposing traffic.

A black man wearing a do-rag hops out of the Nissan, angry, but exposed, and cars blow by him because now instead of an accident victim, he's just someone else in the way. "Move nigga!" a driver yells, and leads several cars in speeding past the man, nearly clipping him. Drivers proceed carelessly as if the black man were nothing. Even the children playing basketball in narrow driveways or double-dutch on the cracked walk have to take pause and step further away from the curb. The black man hops back in his Nissan, slams the door, and drives off. The children resume play, business as usual.

In that moment, the black Nissan driver was one of us. A bird caught in the whirl of a rough city, of drivers speeding up on us when seen in the road, of passersby flinging unfinished food at us, an amalgam of ketchup and mustard and saliva splaying our dark feathers.

Girlfriend leaves us alone. She slows when she sees us, *Come on birds!* she says, drumming the wheel, *y'all got wings, now go!* But she's patient in her own way, she sees us picking crumbs out of the road, going about our business of survival, and she doesn't fault us for that. She just lurches forward in her Honda Accord, some part of her tempted to floor it, knowing we'll take flight and scatter instantly. But I feel her protection, her bleeding heart that refuses to risk hurting us. At least she *thinks* about hitting the brake. She understands that life is fragile—even pigeon life, and grants us some kind of consideration despite how dirty and disease-ridden she knows we are. We make people sick and we know this, and it's a shame we're both so close in proximity yet cast to different worlds.

But still she slows her car for us, and we appreciate the gesture, we consider it a kindness.

Honk! Honk!

Everyone is jamming angry palms into their horns, Boyfriend too, because even though he's the source of the problem, the red Mustang in the middle of the road, he wants the hood to see how big his balls are, how taut with muscle his big manly warrior chest is, how fierce a scowl he can fire toward these motherfuckers who dare challenge him on his stomping grounds, in his hood, and right in front of his girl's house too, his *girl's* house. The disrespect. Complete disrespect. How dare these niggas not respect him. My God. Don't these niggas know that Boyfriend has got to rep his hood? Apparently not. Engines behind him rev hard in rhythmic chorus. *Move! Move! Move!*

All we do in this world is move, that's what life had given us, and even when Boyfriend's not stopping up traffic, I feel very little movement from him anyway, I feel like he would make a bad bird, and I'm glad that there aren't birds like him; I suppose we have wings for a reason.

We wait for someone to tell Boyfriend to move his car, but that's not going to happen. I guess he looks angry enough to instill fear because Boyfriend's big enough and black enough to scare more than just the occasional white passerby. Boyfriend is the-nigga-you-don't-mess-with as the locals often say, the one that gives dark skin the agency to move about the night, as if all dark people suddenly grew powerful when cloaked within hard urban pitch.

Boyfriend steps out of the car, clenching his fists. He glares at the stopped cars and the air suddenly changes.

No more honking. Everything goes quiet.

Cars slowly make their way around Boyfriend as if in apology. I imagine the cars standing on their rear wheels, tip-toeing—tip-*wheeling*—around a really big black man. It occurs to me that maybe he thinks he's moving in life, *going somewhere* as people say, and that he's not moving in actuality because he doesn't perceive a lack of movement. He has a moving problem because his muscle and skin makes things move around him, he's getting what he wants without doing much of anything, at least in the immediate moment.

But for how long?

Girlfriend isn't having any of it, and he knows that. That's why he's here even though she told him not to come back. *Nigga you on Time Out,* she had said, *Time Out. I better not see you for three months, or ever.*

Time Out isn't over, it's been two days, but Boyfriend is here anyway. With some planned brilliance I suppose.

Boyfriend closes his eyes and breathes deep, doing a couple ins-and-outs, something we'd never seen him do before. He reaches a hand into his right pocket, lets the hand linger there for a couple seconds, and takes it out. "Control," I hear him say to himself, "Impulse control, like momma told me. I got this. Impulse. Control." Like the impulse to not do the things we're used to Boyfriend doing. The things that made all the cars apologize to him and his red Mustang, which is still parked in the middle of the road. The things that drew us to Girlfriend's house in the first place—outside of Girlfriend herself—in case Boyfriend got out of line, or out of control, again.

He eyes Girlfriend's door like a target, and steps onto the curb. He advances up the cement path toward her front step; his gait is measured and steady, his back straight and tall, and his face has softened from a scowl to something neutral, a calm expression. He's not slouching or stomping or furrowing his brow like we're used to. He's not being a hoodlum for once; he's promising peace and that makes us nervous. *The quiet before the storm,* people say, and that's true. Our senses are keen and we're gone long before the first drops hit, before the sky goes white with the storm to come.

We clutch our gifts hard, anxious for Boyfriend's next move.

The salamander in my mouth wriggles wildly; it's thrashing in pain, it's screaming and screaming because I almost killed it, but it's alive and that's all that matters, that's all I'm really concerned about. The thing's got fight.

Boyfriend reaches the door and knocks.

"Baby?"

Boyfriend speaks in a deep baritone that nearly rattles the windows. We're waiting for Girlfriend to get home; he thinks she's there. She left dressed in her best, for church and then family time. That's what she does—especially when a nigga isn't acting right. He knocks again.

"Baby? It's me. I know I'm on Time Out and all that craziness but I just wanna tell you that I'm sorry, I apologize from the bottom of me because I know I hurt you tho…I didn't mean to do all that…all that stuff that I did to make you raise up on me like that, I was just having a moment, a bad moment that's all."

Boyfriend starts to look worried. He breathes in, breathes out, and knocks again. Meanwhile Girlfriend's Honda Accord pulls up behind his Mustang. She makes an angry face at the familiar car, but remains stopped, turns her hazard flashers on. She looks out at her doorstep at Boyfriend, speaking from the bottom of him and all. She doesn't say anything, just joins us in our watching, and listens.

"Now, if ya cud just like, tell me what I did, then we'll be straight. We'll be cool and all that and we can get back to all the lovey stuff we be doin' 'cause girl, you really bring out the soft in me, you know, that huggy-feely type nigga that don't come out 'cause momma say she can't pay my *ridiculous* car note and my daddy, well you know how it go… What I do, tho?"

He reaches into his right pocket, leaves his hand there, rolls it around a bit, feeling.

"Seriously tho, how you gonna put a nigga on Time Out and not tell him what he did tho? How can I learn from what I did and what I'm sorry for if you don't guide me into what's right? I just need you there for me so I can be there for you, ya dig? I did things. And you did things, in response, but this response, I don't know babe…it's…it's…it's questionable. Not quite objectionable or anything, not there yet, but it be gettin' there tho."

He waits for a response. Nothing. Girlfriend is still where she's at, listening, losing patience because she takes Time Out seriously. She's flustered even though she's always so tightly in control, and you can see her thinking hard, looking pained because reflection is tough business. As a bird all we have is the sky and our thoughts. We come down for scraps and then fly back up into high white meditation; everything down here is so complicated, it's too much and the people down here do too much, torture themselves by how much they're always doing, even Girlfriend.

Many people down here are actually moving, but often times participate in craziness, and in meditation I wonder: I*s it hard to know how to treat each other? How to take care of one another? We do it, we're hundreds strong, why can't people? Why can't two people do this thing right?*

He pulls his hand out of his pocket, and in his hand there is a condom in a black package with gold lettering: Magnum. He leaves it on her Welcome mat.

"Anyway," he says with a deep smirk carved into his face, "I learned my lesson, and I'm sorry. So yeah, just hit me up babe, when you ready for the, you know, that Make-Up Sex. You know what it is, how we get down. Just call me, I'ma be waitin' wherever I am, in Time Out, ya dig."

He begins to leave and sees Girlfriend in the walkway, pounding toward him angrily.

I look across the telephone wires at my brethren and they're looking back. They're waiting for my signal. So I give it to them: I raise both wings and they go flying.

Girlfriend continues to pound toward him, she's at the curb, she's halfway up the cement path toward her door where Boyfriend waits, smiling widely. His arms are outstretched to receive her in a hug; Girlfriend cocks her fist.

One of our brothers drops his load, the Simply Lemonade bottle-cap he's gifting Girlfriend. It lands between Girlfriend and Boyfriend, bouncing, rattling, and after a couple seconds finally stopping.

They both look up.

Our pigeon brethren are circling above, casting dark moving shadows over the house. Now they're all dropping their special somethings for Girlfriend to have. The drop resembles snow. Pieces of Styrofoam that once contained her favorite Hawaiian Fried Rice, the Asiago Chicken Sandwich wrapper, fortunes she's gleamed at but had thrown away from Chinese places she frequents—all of it floating down slowly, ceremonially, like small white blessings.

Boyfriend goes running because he feels attacked. He flies into his car and yells to Girlfriend, "Go inside! Call me later!" And then winking, "I know you will," and speeds off.

The children playing in the streets, the neighbors walking by, the backed-up cars—all of them disappear, go away and into hiding and such.

Bottle-caps and clips and pins and hair-bows and other gifts we think suit Girlfriend also come flying down. They land around her and she's scared, she's terrified, she looks as if she's about to cry—but that's not something we can help so we keep going. Girlfriend is paralyzed in fear and she's ready to go inside, to shut us out, to reject our goodwill, and as she steps toward her front door she sees the messages on the fortunes peppering the doorway:

It will be alright, allow life to be good to you.

Winning numbers: 7, 23, 5, 38, 10, 12

Happiness is out there, it's closer than you think.

I descend toward Girlfriend, swiftly, with the salamander still thrashing in my mouth. I land before her, impeding her path to the doorway, and we lock eyes, her pupils shimmering with fear, with tears inside she refuses to let go. But she's still here, waiting, giving us the chance that nobody else would.

My brethren continue to circle, dropping gifts.

I lower my beak, reverently setting the salamander down. It's injured, its spine crushed by my grip, but he's managing to crawl toward her, slowly, yet tenaciously. The salamander is crawling and getting closer and he's yells something that I can't understand because it sounds guttural and hurt. But he keeps going, he's not stopping. The salamander is getting closer and closer, he's almost there, he's almost there, he's almost to the tip of her shoe. He yells again and this time it is clear, in our animal tongue he's cries out Girlfriend's name, *Jacq! Jacq!* And even though to her it must register as a low hiss, her eyes soften.

Girlfriend bends down and cups her hand toward the salamander because she knows.

Heather Bell
Forthcoming from *A Horse Made of Fire*, Cobalt Press

Last Will and Testament

In the event of my death,
no autopsy. I am embarrassed of most
of my internal parts. Mosquito-sized
heart, Civil war meat digesting, blood

crawling forward. Please donate
my mother to a hostel in Brazil.
Please take that which is not visible

but scented of flowers and bottle it,
give it to Josiah. Return my car

to the mailman, return my bank account's
balance to the government, return

my bubbling over pots to
the landlord. I guess I will miss

all of you. At my funeral,

give Uncle Harold my left fingerprint,
to help him with his thieving and
romancing of underage girls.

Do not open the chest at the end
of my bed, it is full of

the years in which you spent
looking for yourself in a mirror
and found only a dead person.

My lawyer keeps a swallow in a cage in his
living room. It is wild and I have always
found this to be very cruel,
until this moment.

I am leaving you
because of Tuesday, you remember:

walking in on you at the sink,
pouring boric acid over a mouse you had
captured in a cup. That was my favorite mug,

you know, the one with the witty saying
about life on the side and now

I no longer feel comfortable using
it for coffee,
which has made me feel so hopeless
and tired.

Talea Anderson

A Guide for the Visually Impaired

Among our kind, when seen from afar (though not so far afar), people bear a certain resemblance to fire hydrants. The two share a kind of upright quality, a knobbiness about the head, and neither approaches the curb unless dressed (or painted) in shades of yellow, red, or blue. With experience, however, you might come to understand that fire hydrants, unlike people, stand in one place. What's more, they lie low to the ground, lower than most human beings. These wise observations have probably come to you with time. One fine morning, you prepared a false smile or snippet of empty banter ("Good morning!" etc.), only to find you were addressing the neighborhood hydrant. It happens to even the best of the un-sighted.

The person-hydrant conundrum should well illustrate why one must approach not only sidewalks, but also buses, cars, people, and lost lenses with clear rules in hand. This guide will elaborate a few of these in the pages that follow.

1. Sidewalks

When walking on sidewalks, your primary concern must be to disguise the state of Not-Seeing and Not-Knowing and instead, simulate the state of Wisdom and General Coolness. To begin with, since you cannot see, you will want to memorize your route, for there is nothing more disruptive to the illusion of Wisdom and General Coolness than having to gawp at street signs. Therefore, if you must walk even four blocks to school, plan scrupulously. Draw maps with streets appropriately labeled—one map will suffice for a four-block journey, but for longer journeys to the grocery store or airport, plan on mapping your route multiple times, each with greater precision than the last. This way, if you are confused when leaving your home—if you mix up north with south and walk two miles AWAY from the grocery—you can then consult your largest scale maps, and in this way, determine your position in the city, county, state, or planet, if need be. A casual, absent-minded air will serve you well throughout all of your sidewalk journeys. Think: professorial. You might even carry a briefcase to supplement the illusion. If you're seen lost, crossing and recrossing the same street, people might judge—*But*, if you also look like a half-crazed academic with things to say about string theory and semiotics, people will probably take your behavior for granted. They'll chalk up your confusion to a kind of sweet, endearing forgetfulness, which is really just evidence of your extreme genius. Indeed, when you walk past a friend without recognizing her, you must pretend that an all-absorbing thought is to blame. "Oh!" you'll say after she's said your name, sharply, "Hello!" Your friends will remark that you're forever being caught by surprise, and all of you will laugh about it. "Yeah," you'll say, "I should pay better attention." Amusing as your bumbling ways may be, you can lessen the blow by never looking toward a person when passing him/her/it on the sidewalk. This maneuver—the look—incurs far too much risk, for if you look at a person whom you do not know, and you do not smile at this person, she will be instantly offended. Alternatively, if you opt to smile at all passersby, you risk under-smiling at an acquaintance and over-smiling at a non- acquaintance. Furthermore, you increase the likelihood of being greeted by an Unknown Blur, with whom you will have to simulate a shared knowledge of affectionate experience: "Oh," you'll say. "Hello! So nice to *see* you!" If you're lucky, you'll deduce by the voice that the Unknown Blur is male or female, and from there, you can inquire about Sports or Shopping, as you see fit. All of this can be avoided, however, if you simply peer away from the passing lane of the sidewalk. Adopt an air of deep concentration, as if you are a scientist of abandoned beer bottles, shoe leather, rotting leaves, or—what's that far to the opposite-direction-of-the-passing-person? An atomic blast? Superman?

2. Cars

It's all guesswork, crossing at intersections. You might see a blur in the distance or, when the blurs stop, you'll find yourself face-to-face with these long-nosed, glassy-eyed beasts with whom you share no common language. If you're in an accommodating mood, you might try out a (one-sided) conversation: "Would you like to go first? Or shall I? You? Me? I should go, you say? Alright, then." A little acting will do you good in this situation—you might gesture like Spock greeting earthlings, or Yoda levitating stubborn starships. Pretend you're a queen, all imperious, or Captain Picard, instructing the Enterprise to engage or disengage. The trouble is, you'll never see your audience. You'll never know if they like the show.

When you do cross the street, beware of anthropomorphizing. You might read the rev of an engine as a growl, i.e., anger, and rush to soothe

the bully. Don't bother—once an animal, always an animal. You might as well cross by ear. Listen for the cough and rattle of an oncoming car and if you hear silence, gallop across like a spooked deer. Until electric cars really hit the roads, your odds are pretty good.

If you wish to meet a friend who will drive you somewhere in her car, you must evolve a whole new set of strategies. To begin with, you'll want to work on your language skills. After encountering a car at an intersection, you'll be naturally inclined to say things like, "The Red Blur tried to kill me!" By your taxonomy, cars come in Red, Blue, and White varieties, some with deeper voices than others, but all of the species Car. You'll find, on further investigation, that vehicles go by a complex assortment of names—and further, that some four-wheeled machines are classified in the Truck, Recreational Vehicle, and Gas Guzzler families. You may want to adjust your language accordingly. To discover the truth, press your face close to the make and model of your friends' cars—or invent something. If you mention the "Toyota Infernus" or "Suzuki Samurai" or "GM Native American," no one will be the wiser. You'll look like a car expert.

However, being picked up is a tricky business. Unfortunately, in your world, all Red Cars bear a striking resemblance to each other (it's a world of infinite car-tuplets, all of them identical twins). You will want to select a designated meeting spot—force the Car to find you. Plant your feet at, say, cement marker #3 and hold El Aleph or Labyrinths before your face. If you can think beyond this stomach-turning, white-knuckled vigil of yours, savor the irony of reading, in this moment, the postmodernist ravings of a blind librarian.

If you must move from your perch, you can sidle past some of the identicals and check their license plates (as it turns out, they have numbers to tell them apart!). It may be difficult to read the license plates while still appearing casual—also, you would never want to approach a stranger's car for the license-read. To be clearer, you would never want to make your license-reading intentions known to strangers. It will take some practice, but you must walk coolly—and carefully—through the parking lot, pretending that you've dropped an object beside each car in turn, so that you can position your face near the plates. It's always best, however, to stay still and occupied with such as Borges, while waiting for your ride. You may be tempted to "keep an eye out" for the Correct Car, but it only causes problems when you look at—and fail to recognize—your own father when he drives up. You might lie to him later—tell him that, while you waited, you were developing a mathematical formula for the color of sky. You were formulating the chemical composition of December leaves. You were observing the dumpsters just over his shoulder—just past his car—for an upcoming social sciences class, for a project about the economy of dumpster space as it relates to garbage production in academic settings. In sum, you were distracted.

If you want to avoid the lie, it's always best to wait sloped inward. This way, your father will understand why your face didn't light up for him—why your eyes slipped past him as if he were a tree branch or a speck of gum. It's because you weren't paying proper attention, that's all.

3. Buses

You will become well acquainted with buses, over time. You'll know the anxious counting of streets as you ride along, and the leaning forward, vainly, for a sign. Of course, you're already well aware that you can't read street signs at any distance (an inability that's especially bothersome on buses). You've probably performed your own little circus act on occasion, for your brother or a friend, as you drive across country. It's an old scene, one you've acted out in grade school, high school, and even college: "Tell me when you can read that green sign," your brother might say. "I can read it right now: Camrose, 65 miles." "What green sign?" you ask, peering. "Exactly," your brother says, a little smug, a little amazed. Moments later, you see the sign, but you can't read it until that instant—a split second—when it's passing. You see it over your shoulder. "I saw Camrose!" you say, jubilant.

This kind of slapdash sign-reading will do you no good on the bus. You will have to feel out the driver when you board, see if he's the type to remember your problems or if he's thinking, instead, about the sluggish breaks and the passenger who croaks, "Gollum," over and over, from the front seat. Either way, you'll grip a pole two-handed and wait it out.

Sometimes it's wise to pre-ride your route with a sighted person in tow. A sighted person can tell you to pull the cord when you see the red smudge (Safeway). He can even help you find your house again. Each of these advantages makes a pre-ride worthwhile, but beware when a family member introduces you to the buses. If your father is the first to show you around, he might handle it like a driving lesson—he might even yelp directions at you as if demonstrating the stick-shift to a crash-prone newbie. When the bus arrives at the stop, he'll point to the route number posted on the bus:

"That's how you know which one to board," he'll say.

"I can't see it," you might reply, because you can't. Then he'll walk you to the windshield and put his hand on the number.

"Here. See?"

You do not see, but you demand—urgently, hissing—that he leave the windshield and board the bus like a normal person. Perplexed, he'll try to laugh off the spat. As he enters the bus, he'll apologize to the driver, "She's a little slow."

In this situation, you have two choices:

a) Complete the bus ride in aggrieved silence, an attitude which you will have to break, ultimately, to ask your father when to pull the cord.
b) Muster a fake grin. Comfort yourself in the knowledge that you and your father are both, equally, embarrassed of the other. Assure yourself, furthermore, that, by your seventieth birthday, you will no longer remember this occasion, or care.

4. When Sidewalks Disappear

Of course, you will lose sight of sidewalks at some time in your life. One night, you will perch your glasses beside your bed, only to find, by morning, that they've fallen. Sometime in the night your flailing arm sent them tumbling, just heavily enough to knock a lens loose. You'll feel for the lens with your fingers. You'll try not to panic as you catch sight of it—only just—by the flicker of light on plastic. Then, blind, you will mash the lens in place and, once again, you'll mount your eyes on the bridge of your nose. This is when you find that you have reassembled your glasses incorrectly, and the world is suddenly crooked, leaning, tilted, broken, streaked, and warped—no longer the world you once knew. You will call your parents by feel to request advice, long-distance. When they turn you away, you will fumble through your morning tasks: you press a bottle to your eyes in hopes of telling SHAMPOO from CONDITIONER; you place nose to outlet and—scrabbling a bit—plug the blow dryer into the wall; you pick out an apple by feel, never knowing if it's bruised or green. Your father tells you to visit an optometrist. You wonder how to find the path to his office.

The optometrist or optician or ophthalmologist or eye specialist might try to make you feel that you belong, that you aren't lost at all. When you're young, they'll visit your school with models of the eye and explain everything to your classmates (who prefer to sit in judgment at the monkey bars, calling you Four Eyes—forget the models). The eye doctors show your classmates how pieces of you (of your eyes) are missing; they say that these explanations will build solidarity in the classroom. The eye doctors will invite you to Christmas parties and summer camps for blind children—even bribe you with Barbie dolls, balls-and-jacks. At the parties you'll find blind kids flat on their backs, twitching and drooling and jabbering in not-English. You'll take the Barbie (even though you never liked dolls) and then, once safely home, you'll beg your mother to never make you go back. "Why won't she come?" the doctors wonder. "These are her people."

Someday, the special needs people may show you Sound and Fury, to teach you about disabilities and belonging. Of course, this documentary is about the deaf, not the blind—but you won't mention it. They'll just say you're all alike.

From the documentary, you will learn about two deaf parents who must decide whether to allow their daughter (also deaf) cochlear implants. With the implants, she might hear again, at least a little. In one scene, the girl's father signs to his hearing parents that he will not give his daughter implants because he wants her to appreciate "deaf culture."

"Deaf culture?" his parents ask, not bothering to sign it. "Deafness isn't 'culture.' It's a curse, a thing to overcome. How could you do this to her?"

The father replies in sign. He is swaying in agitation but he is silent save for the popping of hand against hand as he signs fast and hard. His teeth are clacking open and shut but he voices nothing. He's like a dolphin out of water, its jaws clicking uselessly in the air. His parents can't read his signs and, indeed, he is saying that they don't understand. He worked all his life to be understood by hearing people. He learned to read his parents' lips with 35% accuracy, learned to pantomime at family reunions. He did all of that, but he won't give up his daughter.

You'll conclude from this that the deaf man's parents had it right. There is no culture in blindness. You're living on a knife's edge—just short of falling on the sidewalks to lie flat and confused on the ground. This is why you must follow the rules. Always you must keep to the script.

5. Exercises for Advanced Learners

If you wish to increase your skill level, you might take some additional chances while walking your sundry routes. For instance, though it is incredibly risky, you might try looking toward the people you pass on sidewalks. Tilt your head to the side so that you're almost looking at passersby and almost not. Smile mildly enough that friends will mistake your smirk for recognition and strangers, for general day-time cheer.

Remember, this skill is extremely difficult to master. When staring into the blurry middle-distance, you'll have a tendency to look grim, or a little confused—definitely not cheerful.

On occasion, you might notice, in that instant when people pass—like road signs, just readable at the last second—that many of them are peering into their hands. They are texting or phoning, eyes down. Sometimes, you might wonder if these sighted people really see each other at all. If not, the worst of it is, they're missing a great performance.

Jay Geigley
2014 Zora Neale Hurston Fiction Prize Finalist

After the End of the World as We Knew It: A Walkthrough

It will be one hundred and ten days after you heard Buck's fiancée Hannah got shot and all he could do was cradle her as she bled out in his arms. It will be one hundred and five days after Hannah's wake, where Buck stood in a suit and shook hands, stonefaced, but unleashed his arms to swallow you, his trusty sidekick, in a crushing hug. It will be ninety-eight days after Buck, still silently grieving, put forth the invitation to come with him to the woods to learn to survive out in the wilderness he grew up in. It will be seventy-six days after the cheap compass, which Buck said he could find North without, started spinning out of control, a sign to Buck, whose dad had prepared his whole life for such a thing, of a solar flare that fried everything with a charge, leaving the world in a forced stone age. It will have been sixty-one days since Buck led the way to the underground survival bunker, built by his dad who never lived to see its use, and locked the door behind you both.

Sixty-one days will have passed entirely within the bunker's hexagonal rooms laid out like a honeycomb, three rooms wide (A-C) and four rooms long (1-4), every doorknob a bank-vault style wheel, all walls the color of spicy mustard. Room A1, the communications room, will be where hundreds of hours were spent listening to static recorded from various channels on the radio, hoping to hear someone out in that technology-free world who's discovered the ability to project a signal. In C4, the firing range, Buck will be impressed by your ability to get a kill-shot on two targets, blindfolded, while he shouts in your ears.

In B2, the rec room, the heavy bag will get pummeled beyond the point of total fist-numbness, and Buck will teach grappling, ending nearly every time with him pinning you to the ground, arm twisted behind your back, but not before you've learned something. The rec room is where Buck will be on the sixty-second day, doing pushups on his fists, lowering his body with a five-count, hissing out his massive lungs, and pressing himself back up, as he does every morning.

Don't look directly at his shirtless sweatiness, the drops of sweat matting down the reddish hair over his back, shoulders and arms, like he's something born of the wilderness and meant to amble naked through the world hurling pieces of it as he wishes.

Stop thinking things like that about a man, the one who saved your life.

Don't ever let him know what the sight of him does to your pulse.

Remember: this bunker isn't big enough to hold two grown men and a bunch of butterfly poetry.

When Buck is done he'll stand up, slightly stooped over (the low, smooth ceilings a few inches below his full six and a half foot stature). He'll ask if you've worked out yet. No matter the response he'll just walk off wordlessly. Just do the workout: five-hundred pushups, five-hundred situps, five-hundred pullups. It will take about an hour, which will be a vast improvement since the first day in the bunker.

Buck will eat breakfast in the dining cell, C3, sitting at the five-sided oak table shaped exactly like the room. He'll have an extra MRE ready in the seat next to his. Tear open the nitrogen-puffed aluminum pillows and think of how sickening the mediciney grape-flavored sugar drink and ammonia-tinged chicken stew were at first, how they actually made the campfire-roasted squirrel and berry-mash from the time out in the woods seem like an appetizing alternative. Try to picture things like lobster mac and cheese or blueberry muffins. They'll feel like things a kid dreamt up.

Buck will sit up straight, his head thick as a cube pressed into his wide shoulders, and say that the bunker's batteries haven't reached full charge in a few days. "I think something damaged the solar panels," he'll say adding that he's going outside to investigate. There will be no invitation to join him. This will be the first time he's mentioned going outside since the bomb-proof door first slammed shut. He'll say, "It could be wildlife, or weather, or degraded materials, or the mechanism that makes them retractable snagged on something. I'm going to take a look, see if I can fix it."

It will be okay to linger outside his room as he prepares for the errand, but try to make it look casual. He'll pack a small toolbox and a hunting knife. He'll grab a heavy jacket, since autumn will have come in the world outside. He'll pack his hunting knife and grab the shotgun he calls Bessie Mae and pack some shotgun shells in his bag. "Maybe I'll come back with some bear meat," he'll say with a wink, holding the shotgun in his fist like it's a club.

He'll leave through a maintenance exit, a tunnel he'll point out for the first time, hidden behind a painting in plain everyday sight of a US Marine choking the grim reaper. He'll look sturdy and unkillable, a true mountain man. Think of a man made of mountain. Feel all that pride for him, just like years ago watching him strike men like a meteor on the football field. Ignore that feeling floating about, like reverse deja vu, like this moment is something that will never happen again.

When the tunnel goes quiet his absence will be everywhere, like everything is a slightly different color with him gone. Replace the painting and head to A4, the library. Grab a puzzle from the stack—a thousand-piece picture of an eagle dragging the American flag through a blue sky—and dump it out on the table, picture side down. Click a stopwatch and nimbly join the pieces, just like every other day in the bunker.

When puzzle-Zen sets in, don't be surprised to feel guilt over missing Buck, but not once for mom, or Jennifer, or Ben from work. They probably didn't make it, but it was easier because they weren't around to say goodbye to when the shit hit the fan.

Remember: the sun flaring, planes falling from the sky, subways crashing in darkness, hospitals blacking out, the internet evaporating, every human suddenly isolated and powerless. Remember imagining the chaos, worldwide, with no way for anyone to make it stop. Remember the quiet of the woods that night, watching a falling star and wondering if it was a satellite plummeting to earth.

The narrow escape from being in the center of that madness was thanks entirely to Buck's sudden desire to retreat to the woods to teach how to live without society, just a few miles away from the spot where Buck's lunatic dad had built a magnetically shielded backup plan for exactly that kind of disaster. It's okay to think warmly back to that time: learning from Buck how to find east by tracing shadows, and how to stun a rabbit with a rock. Remember how shameful it felt to have privately wished to stay in the woods with Buck forever.

When the puzzle is finished, click the stopwatch: 4 minutes, 2 seconds, a new record. Nice work, but it won't count because no one was there to see it.

Head to the communications room and pass time by listening through the tapes while the radio morse codes H-O-W-D-Y on ten different frequencies. Finding other survivors will seem like a worthwhile goal, but Buck will constantly bring up that anyone else still out there will have struggled much more than two men cozy in an EMP shielded home with lights and warmth and running water. He'll insist on staying in the safety of the bunker as long as possible, training.

Remember: after the shit hits the fan, the only people who will survive are those who have and those who are willing to take.

The static will suddenly cut out. Realize what this means, and slowly rewind the tape. Listen to it again, this time at regular speed: the static will suddenly break into silence followed by a deep voice calmly saying,

"Little pigs, let us in." Play it again and listen, ear hairs tingling. Think of the broken solar panels. Think of Buck outside, alone.

Pack a bag with a nine-millimeter, some ammo, and a small first aid kit. It will take a little over a minute. Move the marine-choking-reaper painting and climb through the dusty shaft. Inch along it like a worm, dragging the small pack along with your feet.

At the end, climb the ladder going straight up about fifty feet. On the way up, take a long look at the thick glassy orange layers surrounding the bunker like an internal shell: electromagnetic pulse shielding, which protected the interior of the bunker when the sun's belch caused "The End of the World as We Knew It". At the top of the ladder throw open the hatch, which will be camouflaged on the other side as a rock. Climb out into sunlight. The air outside will be sickening at first, overwhelming with organic smells, moving air, headrush-inducing freshness. Hundreds of colors outside the limited scheme of the bunker will spark from all sides at a level of brightness that can't be controlled with a dimmer switch. Sunglasses would help, but they would reflect and attract attention.

Don't be overwhelmed. Don't feel helpless and inadequate. Fight the loneliness that hasn't existed in months. Shove yourself to your feet and move like a survivor.

Head to where the solar panels are supposed to be. They'll be smashed to pieces. Comb the surrounding woods. Make sure to zig-zag and cover your tracks. As the sun starts to set, about a half-mile away some footsteps will lie stuttered along the ground. Use those tracking skills. Pause, crouch to inspect, and then covertly follow them a few clicks through the trees, right to the person who made them.

It will be a boy with a man-sized body but a face that's only now learning to shave. "Holy shit! I didn't know there were people alive out here!" he'll say. He'll be wearing boots, a heavy brown jacket, and thick gloves, carrying a sledgehammer but using it as a walking stick. He'll march forward with a hand out-stretched. "What's your name guy?"

Draw the nine millimeter and have it trained on him. It will take one second flat, a movement as natural as yawning. Resist the heart pulsing in your ears and the urge to let your ass-cheeks clench.

"Easy, fella," he'll say, setting his sledgehammer down. "My name's Clyde. I don't live far from here either! Are you folks stranded out here?"

Tell him, "It's just me." Say something like, "I just got lost. I've been staying away from the riots in the cities since the shit hit the fan and I've been out here for..." Pretend you don't know exactly what day it is: "Jesus, what's the date?"

"October 26th!" he'll say, getting close enough to lay a big kiss if he wanted. It will be a bad sign that he's not backing down from the gun.

Realize this situation is not under control. "How long have you been out here? You know it's all over, right? I'm part of a rescue team out here trying to pick up stragglers."

Think of the voice that whispered out of the radio and consider that it might have been his. Keep an eye on him but keep scanning the area for others.

He'll say, "Buddy, did you even know? It was an attack by the North Koreans. Some kind of bomb that made stuff go haywire. But we beat 'em and it's over!"

Don't believe him. Remember: it was a solar flare, a Coronal Mass Ejection, something scientists knew would happen eventually, something Buck's dad had planned on for years.

Ask him why he's got a sledgehammer.

He'll say, "There's bears out here!"

There's no reason to believe this kid, but it will be hard not to imagine things going back to the way they were, the end of the world fading like a bad dream.

Ask some questions, like, "Where are the others? Where do you come from? How far is safety?" Don't let willingness to buy this kid's story soften your stance. Don't let your rear leg bend. Don't relax the arm holding your nine.

Then he'll point behind you and say, "Is that big guy back there with you?"

Turn around, take a look into the woods for just three seconds—any longer would be stupid. It will still be too long. The air will whistle and a spring will uncoil in your skull, eyes feeling like they just got pounded back and swallowed. Hot wet blood will pour down your face, heart pounding like a bass drum in each temple, pain coming from the air itself.

There will be no strength to the effort, but still try to resist as "Clyde" slips flexicuffs over your hands behind your back and takes the gun.

Remember: after the shit hits the fan, the only people who will survive are those who have, and those who are willing to take.

Listen to the sound of the zipper on the bag as "Clyde" starts going through it, pocketing the ammo, bouncing the first-aid kit off your head and into the woods.

Feel that hard poke in the skull from behind. It's a gun barrel. "Clyde" in his best tough-guy growl will say, "If you want to live, take me to where you keep your supplies."

Struggle to think through the ringing ears. Talk back, even though the words will bubble out through blood pouring down: "I don't know, I don't—"

He'll press the barrel harder and say, "We know there's another one of you out here and there's a dozen of us. We know you've got a powered-up shelter, now take me to it."

Only two immediate options will come to mind, since surrendering the bunker would never be one of them: either reach deep into the hope that Buck is out there, near, with his gun trained on "Clyde" about to end his life, or decide that this is it, and the bullet about to blast from the nine millimeter will head straight into the ground after it's torn through skull and brain and forehead. Wait for the most significant moments of life to flash by, or to be overcome by calmness and peace. Neither will happen. Just mash your bloody face into the moist ground and hope the pain is brief.

Then there will be a pop off in the woods, another pop from a different direction. The second pop, louder, deeper, will have come from a shotgun. "Clyde" will back away suddenly, his attention trained on the sounds from the rest of the woods.

As he turns, shuffle around and face up, arms sliding down and under until they're in front, hands apart so that the flexicuffs are tight against the wrists. "Clyde" will assume no immediate threat from his captive and take several steps toward the sound of the shots, gun pointed at the ground.

With arms overhead, pull down and back so the cuffs strike your ribs and your elbows go behind. The flexicuffs will break off, just like Buck taught you. There will only be a few seconds to act.

Grab the sledgehammer.

"Clyde" will turn as the sledgehammer comes down on his skull, which will break like wet pottery as it knocks him flat to the ground. He'll lie there, moaning, his limbs twitching, the nine millimeter out of his hands. Bring the sledgehammer down on his head as hard as possible.

Take a moment to reflect on becoming a murderer.

He'll be splattered all over, so wipe him off quickly and grab the nine-millimeter. Search him. He'll have nothing on him but the ammo, so take that back. There will be another pop through the trees behind so head forward, crouched low, gun drawn. Ignore the dizziness, the blood and adrenaline drooling out your head wound.

Crest the hill and look down. A grey-haired man in a leather jacket will have a rifle aimed at Buck, who'll be kneeling on the ground, weaponless and bloody but fists clenched, smiling defiantly at the bullet about to come his way.

Control the sphincter, find the target and squeeze the trigger.

Thattaboy.

The geezer's head will cock suddenly to the left and he'll crumple to the ground. Scan the area. There will be another body fifteen feet to your eleven o'clock, its neck ending in a splintered pulpy mess, but nobody else alive within sight. Jog down the hill toward Buck. Just bear with those wild feelings from seeing him and saving him. He'll slowly rise. Check out the bullet wound on his right thigh. He'll squeeze his teeth into a fierce grin as he tries to put weight on that leg. Still, he'll ask, "You okay bud?"

Tell him what happened: "Guy hit me with a sledgehammer," and scoop a handful of the blood running down your face and look at it. Tell him what happened to "Clyde" though: "I smashed his head like a fucking pumpkin." Buck will smile, his teeth now purple with blood from a recently torn pulpy gap in his front teeth. He'll limp a few feet toward his fallen shotgun and yank it from the ground.

Buck will say, "They've been holed up miles from here, stealing to survive. They heard our signal and saw our solar panels and wanted to loot our supplies. They were trying to lure us out. You should've stayed below."

The next words will burst out so don't even try to resist: "I couldn't let you die without me." Just deal with the nakedness once it's said. There won't be time to retract or explain it. Shouts will come from the woods all around you.

Buck will say, "Back to back. Shoot anything that moves." The shadows of the trees will be spreading and natural light will be retreating.

There won't be much time left. Say some prayers, make quick peace with God, and get ready to kill some people.

Press up against Buck's solid mass like he's a barricade and slowly rotate, gun drawn. The first sign of movement will be at your one o'clock, as a young woman, looking like a new librarian but for the pistol in her hand, steps out of the woods with you in her gunsight.

Remember: shoot for the eye, so the bullet doesn't ricochet off the skull.

Fire one perfect shot and become a murderer for the third time that day.

Bessie Mae will boom once from the other side of Buck, then again. Listen to the trees blasted apart, a man's cry cut short and the sound of wet meat hitting the ground. Smell the gun-powder, the metallic stink of innards, Buck's familiar sweat.

There won't be time to say what hasn't been said.

Don't tell him you love him. That'll be like admitting you're going to die. Let him think you believe you're going to get out of this. Let him believe he taught you to survive.

Thank him, in those last few seconds, silently at least, for choosing you to save, for teaching you to be strong, for making sure you went through none of this alone.

After a pop and a crack, a hot spray from above your head will splatter forward and down. Feel Buck's body, one last time, as he tenses, then falls to the ground slowly like a leaf. When he's down there will be no cover, so take aim and start ending some lives. Let the woods fade away. See only targets, like in the firing range. Howl like an animal until a bullet from behind bursts right through your chest. The breathless feeling, wind knocked out, will come from a punctured lung collapsing. The sudden drop in blood pressure will cause every limb to buckle to the ground but it will spike again and you'll sit right back up. With a wet wheeze take aim and fire every bullet left. One coming back at you will bury itself in your forehead. Watch the sky through the trees as it all darkens. Buck will be the ground beneath you, both of you dead in the same woods where he taught you how to live.

Timothy Liu

Romance in a Red State

I pluck the maraschino
out of your Manhattan—
tie the stem into a knot
with my tongue, feel that
charge when you grab
the burnt uneaten toast
off my breakfast plate
in that roadside redneck
bakery and shove it in
your mouth when it's clear
you've had enough to eat
but still want something
held between us—a secret
smeared across your lips
while everyone else closes
out their tabs, tips their
servers generously or not,
unaware how things go on
right under their noses
all the time, the way you
twirl my Pilot G2 pen
round and round, clicking
the ball point in and out
before pocketing the thing
I thought didn't belong
to you—telling me how
poppers dull the meat
that sometimes punishes
your hole, numbs the ache
you don't want taken
away, not without asking.

Timothy Liu

Unsleeping, 5:03 AM

You make me feel
too much. Don't care
if you're already married,
if your spouse knows
how to lick bone china
clean. As if everything
stunk of meat. I wait
on the curb for someone
to explain why it feels
so wrong to be here
with a plastic bag over
my head, not knowing if
I have a name, not unless
you call—your voice
barreling down on me
like an ice cream truck
with its pre-recorded
Pavlovian song ringing
while I play dead in
the middle of the road
and I have no pocket
change, no job, how is it
you make me feel
like I'm nine years old,
like I haven't yet come
inside a sleeping bag
filled with feathery down
as I rub against another
boy, my asshole sore
from fingering myself
all night, thinking of you—

Tom Williams

The Last Original Guitar Riff in G

Our work doesn't bring us to the suburbs much. In my nearly six years with Containment, it's mainly been recording studios, along with hotel suites and villas in Jamaica or the south of France, or an occasional surprise backstage at a nightclub when only the elite know that So-and-So is testing some new numbers. But on this bright summer afternoon, when Haines stops the van outside a three, maybe four-bedroom ranch that looks like all the houses around it except for the paint on the shutters, it's like I've been transported to the neighborhood I lived in when I was in high school, where my biggest concern was whether I'd be platooning at end with David Dean or he'd play all four quarters.

Of course, I don't tell Haines any of this as we exit the van. He's got me beat by ten years in the Unit. He came on early enough to hear the stories from the first crews, those who'd been around when things were getting started in the fifties. I follow him down the sidewalk, silent, shading my hand over my eyes from the sun. Just like Fountainview Estates in 1984, the trees here haven't grown to do much more than make navigating the push-mower difficult. An oil stain in the shape of Africa mars the driveway. We both avoid it, then step over the bike angled across the porch. I know little about Haines beyond what he's told me about his life in the Unit and his life in it, along with what I can see in his wrinkled face, his high and tight that would still pass Corps muster, his gray suit, white shirt and black tie that match mine. Where was he born? What did he listen to when he was in school? Why is all this coming to me now?

Haines stops, holds a finger to his lips and points to the house. It takes me a minute but I can hear a guitar above the noise of squabbling siblings, wheezing garage doors, and roaring Weed Eaters. Just one guitar, playing the same few notes over and over, unaccompanied, sometimes cleanly, other times not. "Sounds like a Fender copy with a—" Haines pauses, squints. "Peavey. Definitely a Peavey."

I nod, though I wouldn't disagree even if I knew enough to. Haines is at the door in a blink, knocking. Not too hard. We aren't the ATF or

DEA. In fact, when this job came down from the head office, the recommended dress code was that we look like salesman. We needed to blend in and get to this street—what is it Cherry, Maple, Elm?—and get there fast, considering the potential of what was happening inside. I'm even carrying a sample case to complete the disguise, pretending to struggle though it's empty.

Nobody answers the door, and the guitar keeps playing, now moving on to what sounds like the Stones or maybe the Who—I'm always mixing them up, which Haines can't believe: "Do you even own a CD?" he's always asking. Now the amp's turned up a few notches and fuzzed out more than earlier. Haynes looks at his watch. I say, "Reminds me of home" and turn around to salute a rippling flag anchored to a house across the street.

"May I remind you that we're on the clock," Haines says, then knocks again, shifting from a couple of knuckles to a fist.

The guitar stops. There's a hammering of feet on the floor. It sounds like laminate underfoot—surely no developer or homeowner would have laid hardwoods here. Locks get undone on the other side and the person who answers is just a kid. This shouldn't surprise me. It's a summer day. School's out. Maybe he hasn't got a job at McDonald's or his shift doesn't start until later. Still, we never see kids when we're working. The youngest I've encountered was the twenty-two-year-old with the spiky blue hair and cheek tattoo who agreed he would, as Haines suggested, mute the power chords a little more on the next album. But he and his band had sold over ten million units and we were outside his Austin mansion with the swimming pool shaped like an angry fist flipping off the world. It was hard to think of years as the way to measure him.

Holding open the door now, though, is really a kid, maybe sixteen, his mustache scant and his eyes sleepy, his hair a tangled mess like he woke only minutes ago. In Recon, I was trained to size people up quickly, know everything from ethnicity to which is their strong hand or where might they hide a weapon. You expect everyone to be white in a neighborhood like this, like mine, but I can't figure this kid out. Mixed, I'm thinking, though I can't figure out all the parts. If he was the one playing the guitar, experience tells me he's likely part white. But none of this matters for now. Haines has started his spiel: "We were wondering if we might interest you in a product guaranteed to make your life 100 percent easier."

The kid's hanging on the door, his arm elongated and his mouth open. He doesn't say anything but he pulls the door wider and that's all Haines needs. He's through and I follow. We don't need to get physical—the main reason I'm here—but I flex my biceps and swivel around my neck just in case. "What's in the case, dude?" the kid says, and I pause, remembering to hoist it like something's actually inside. The kid's eyes close again.

"Say," Haines says, "what was that CD you were listening to before?"

This gets the kids eyes open. He gazes at my sample case, but doesn't notice it's just about as tall as he is. He says, "What CD?"

"Sounded like some pretty good guitar on it."

Haines knows what he's doing. I'm surprised. You deal with rock and roll guys as much as he does, he might have lost his touch with someone this young. The kid's smile is brief, but I see it, and I wish I'd seen the color of his gums to have a better idea just what he is. He says, "That was me." He digs a hand out of his pocket, wipes his mouth. "I was playing." He cocks his head. He nods at the sample case. "What are you trying to sell?"

"I don't believe it," Haines says. "That was you?" He shakes his head. A smile as false as a promise tightens his creased face. He says, "Prove it."

The kid's smile is back, as legit as Haines's isn't. "Follow me."

It doesn't take him long to get to the room, which is as messy as mine was when I was his age, only instead of dirty clothes, shoulder pads and a helmet and *Sports Illustrateds* with Elway and Marino on the covers, his mess is made by heavy metal magazines, occasional rap ones, too, and jeans that all look like they'd fit Haines and me at the same time. I loosen my tie, undo a button, blocking the doorway while Haines clears off some space and sits on the unmade double bed. The kid plugs back in. I'll be damned if the guitar isn't a Fender copy and the amp has PEAVEY spelled out in silver on the front. And he's banging out those same few notes, futzing a few of them but starting to get his timing down, and then, on the fourth try, playing each note so it rings like a coin dropped in an empty can and staring at Haines as if to say *I told you.*

Haines is off the bed and clapping before the kid can say anything. "Man, that's good stuff," Haines says. "Too good." Then he stops clapping and turns to me, nods. The kid still smiles when I grab the neck of the guitar but his mouth and eyes both widen when I yank away his instrument. Next it's his skinny arm, and I spin it behind his back. "Don't resist," I say. "It's easier that way."

•

On the drive back to the airport, Haines apologizes for the rough treatment and the short time the kid spent inside the sample case. He gives him the history during the flight, how, back in the fifties, the Unit was formed with the belief that this crazed teenage music, rock and roll, was not just a passing phase but a serious threat to social order that had to be contained. Not *eliminated*, Haines emphasizes, as there were individuals and corporations even as early as fifty-eight who'd figured out ways to profit from all the screeching, while containing it in a way that keeps it from becoming a truly transgressive moment in human history. Haines likes that last phrase. He's said it every time we've been on such a call, and there are times when I think he believes it. But as he goes on, and the kid finally seems awake enough to understand, I stop listening. I've heard it before, plus I've never quite figured out how it's all supposed to work or why it was determined around sixty-two that, by having British bands play essentially the same music that black guys did in the fifties, there would no longer be any of the interracial mixing that had frightened so many. I mean, I do and I don't understand, for here's exhibit a, the kid, of people of different races getting together. Yet there's my own recollection of every concert we've gone to, Haines and me, and how the only black people at rock and roll shows are security. Things might be a little different at the rap and R&B concerts, but that's not my area. I'm also confused about how the Unit operates, being both, as Haines says now (so I am listening, after all), above and within the government, here and abroad. Whatever the case, the checks don't bounce so I do what I'm asked, which on this afternoon is to secure this kid's transit to somewhere no one would know how to find him.

Haines is done with his story. I look at the kid and he's nodding but in the way I used to nod to older people, hopeful that doing so would make sure this endless story was over. Haines pats him on the knee. "Understand what I'm saying then?"

The kid nods but as quickly shakes his head. He says, "This is about music." He looks my way, flinches. His hand rises to knead his right shoulder. "Right?"

A signal flashes above the door to the cockpit. We'll be landing soon. Haines says, "Shit, I don't even know your name, buddy."

I lean in closer, hoping to hear a name like LaMarcus or Jesus or Ban. "Jake," the kid says, which even a bachelor like me knows is a popular boy name of the last decade. I quit. This is why I'm in Containment, not Inquiry, like Haines's buddy Rothschild, who tipped us off about this one in the first place. The plane's begun its descent, and I see Jake start at the angle. I wonder if it's his first time on a plane.

We rarely get this far. Most of the performers in the business, they've been indoctrinated by somebody—a manager, record exec, a fellow performer—and we're reminders, not enforcers. Oh, there's been a few I've heard of who wouldn't turn it down or switch to country or gospel or movie soundtracks. There's a famous left-hander from Seattle, Haines says, who everybody thinks is dead but is really hanging out in this very unit, ordering pizzas from Domino's and getting fat as a tick. But Jake's too young, which is why we're this far into the call. He doesn't know enough to know better, and Haines tells me now, as we watch the kid sitting in an interrogation room that looks as swank as a hotel suite in Manhattan, that's what makes this particular job so difficult. "I can't tell," Haines says. "Which way he's going to go." On the other side of the glass, Jake picks up a pack of Marlboros—which seems to me a sign that he's mostly white—then looks around and pockets the pack, as if saving them for later.

"What happens if he says no?" I say.

"He stays."

Jake's probably a lazy little fucker who regularly slept past noon, talked back and kept up his family by playing too loud and too late, but he had to have people who might miss him. "Jesus, Haines," I say. "What about his family?"

"They get this." And he pulls out of the inside pocket of his jacket a folded piece of paper, which has, "Dear Mom and Dad," at the top and "That's why I don't want to come back home," right before his forged signature. "Kids go missing all the time. For real," Haines says when I hand back the letter. He smacks the paper against his hand. "And Christ, did you hear that riff? It was going to blow shit up." I wonder who turned Jake in, if it was a friend or a neighbor or a teacher or a family member. Or maybe the Unit already has the monitoring device Haynes keeps talking about on every guitar sold. "I guess so," I say, but I'm not convinced. Then again, what do I know about music? Haines is right. I don't even own a CD. On the radio I recognize a song or two, mostly ones on the oldies station that we listened to before games to get riled up. Stuff to chant and bang on shoulder pads to, but little else.

"I'm going to need you inside," Haines says. He looks right at me. "It might get to that point."

That point is a place I've never been in this job, at which I'm more than just the threat of being physical. I might actually have to cuff the kid around or make absolutely certain that he won't ever be able to do anything on the guitar again. I stare at my hands. They've been there to take out who knows how many enemies back in the Gulf, but haven't been one on one since I was trying to beat out David Dean for starting defensive end. "Just look," Haines says, and sure enough Jake is walking in the direction of the guitar and the amp. They're not hidden, exactly, but kept in a place where someone would have to look for them. This, Haines tells me, demonstrates just how important playing is to the person involved. That alone isn't dangerous, but what Jake does next is: he plugs in and bangs out that riff, which, now that I'm listening, is pretty catchy. Haines says, "Follow me," and I do.

It's probably the best guitar that Jake has ever played. The Unit never scrimps, and coming through the amp that's nearly as tall as the lanky little fucker—I had to tuck his legs to fit him in that sample case—I'm really hearing what the kid's playing and catch myself humming along as we walk in. Haines shouts, "Jake, could you turn it off for a minute?"

Jake nods but he rakes the volume knob higher and smacks the fat blue pick against the strings once more, really knocking it out. The sound is filling the empty spaces in me—between my ribs, behind my knee-caps—and moving me forward more than I am. Haines yanks the amp's plug out of the wall. "That's better," he says. He's smiling again, though Jake's probably figured out enough to mistrust it. "How did you come up with that riff?" Haines says.

Jake needs a second to realize the volume is gone. He keeps playing and I wonder how loud the sound is in his head. He pockets the pick—little klepto—and rubs his chin against the torn collar of his t-shirt. "I was trying to play La Bamba," he says.

"Why play that spic music?" Haines says, and I wonder if he's trying to figure out the same thing that I am. I stand near the door, even though it's locked, my knees bent slightly, my hands damp and pressed against my sides.

Jake says, "That's not cool." But that's it. Nothing more. No curse words in Spanish or defense of his mother or father's race. "Your generation is so out of touch."

"So I am, so I am," Haines says. He sits down on the sofa across from Jake. At last, the kid takes the guitar off and leans it against the amp. Haines says, "You understand then that my friend here and I aren't just music lovers. That we're here to make sure that you and that riff don't go anywhere where you might do some serious societal damage?"

"Why do you care?" Jake says, defiant.

"Why don't you just make it easy on yourself, Jake," Haines says. "Just put the guitar down. Go back home. Have fun and dick around with your garage band or whatever. Just don't play that riff in G anymore." He leans closer. He's not smiling now. "Ever."

"This is a joke, right? This is, like, totally un-American." He looks at me and winces again. My palms grow even damper, like they're feeling the guilt the rest of me is trying to ignore.

"Listen up, Jake," Haines says. "You're not the first person we've had here. You won't be the last."

"Like who?"

His eyes glaze over as Haines mentions some of the people the Unit has silenced or convinced to invest their efforts elsewhere, but a few make the poor kid wince. He's shaking his head by the time Haines mentions that famous left-handed player, and Jake says, "He's dead, man. I read two fucking books about him."

"Oh no, he's right in here. Blows away everybody in Rock Band, on drums and vocals, too. You can meet him right before we leave. After you promise to quit playing that riff."

For a long minute, Jake just stares at the guitar leaning against the amp. It's cherry red and shines so bright I can see the blurry reflection of Jake's long face. His fists bounce on his shaking knees. I still don't know just what he is and won't until I ask him, but the way he seems now and with his memory of my sleeper hold, why would he say anything to me. When he stands and walks toward Haines, I relax, pretty certain that, like all the rest, he's about to say that, in the end, a few cool notes don't mean that much. And after Haines stands and extends his hand, Jake nods. Their hands get pretty close before Jake wheels around, plugs in the amp, straps on the guitar, and jacks every knob up to such a volume that my teeth are rattling before he even strikes a note. Which he does, of course, hammering that riff out so cleanly it sounds like a recording from the most up to date studio around. Only this time, he's got more. Rather than playing the riff over and over, he slides into a little solo, then some chords, his fingers forming the shapes while he stares directly at Haines. If he's got words yet, he's not sharing them now, but Haines has this to say to me: "It's that time." And my hands free themselves from my sides before I even think. Yet I want to watch this kid play. "Goddam it," Haines says. "It's time."

I don't remember a single moment like the one when I learned my football career would end. No members of a covert agency visited me to make that clear. There was just this moment when the lack of recruiting letters from even the tiny colleges and the shrinking playing time made it pretty certain that soon I would be turning in my equipment for a last time. When I take the few steps toward Jake and he keeps playing, I know I should have in mind the fracture of a couple of fingers on both hands so they'll never glide so easily over these strings again. Yet I can't. Haines says my name twice and slaps me on the shoulder but he quiets when I get his left hand behind his back—I knew he was a portsider after our first five minutes together—and it's almost like he knows what I'm doing when I put him in the hold, like he maybe approves. The sight of Haines crumpled on the couch finally gets Jake to stop playing, but before he says a word I hand him the cash in my wallet and combine that with what's in Haines's. "Eight hundred," I say. "Plenty to get back home."

"Why?" Jake says, the guitar still strapped to him, like it should never come off.

I shrug, say, "Get out of here," and guide him back to my empty sample case. It's a tight fit, sure, but when we're off the base and he's on his way to the airport to fly home I finally feel as though I come to, thinking that I have a decision of my own to make now and need to get moving. But already I can hear Jake's song in my head. I don't know if he's got words of his own or needs to meet the person who's going to supply them. Either way, it's playing in my head now, like it's on the radio, on the way to a Friday night game, when everything seemed on the verge of changing for the better.

Contributors

Talea Anderson holds a BA in history and creative non-fiction writing from Walla Walla University, an MLIS from the University of Washington, and an MA in history from Central Washington University.

Carrie Bistline is a gregarious closet nerd with an MFA in Creative Writing. This starving artist is a mixture of planned spontaneity, disorganized efficiency, and perfectionistic procrastination.

Ryan W. Bradley is the author of four chapbooks, three poetry collections, a story collection, and a novel, *Code for Failure*. His latest book is a novella called *Winterswim*.

Wes Civilz writes poems and stories, and is at work on his memoir about lust. He also makes video art on YouTube.

Anne Colwell received two fellowships from the Delaware State Arts Council, three fellowships to the Bread Loaf Writers Conference, and has published two books of poetry, *Believing Their Shadows* and *Mother's Maiden Name*.

Cara Cotter, from Buffalo, NY, received her MFA in 2013 from University of New Orleans. Her work has appeared in Canisius College's *Quadrangle*, but this is her first professional publication.

Liz Dolan's *A Secret of Long Life*, nominated for the Robert McGovern Prize and a Pushcart, was published by Cave Moon Press. Her first collection, *They Abide*, was published by March Street.

Leslie Doyle lives in New Jersey. Her fiction has appeared in *Clapboard House*, *Front Porch*, *Down and Out*, and *Wind Journal*. She teaches at Montclair State University.

Gabriel Fushong lives with his wife Lauren in Missoula, MT. He is an avid baseball fan and proud member of Cardinals nation, having joined the flock at the urging of his grandfather in the mid-80s.

Jay Geigley is a recent graduate of the MFA writing program at the University of New Hampshire and an amateur bodybuilder. This is his first published story, and thus his first bio.

Poet Laureate of San Antonio, **Laurie Ann Guerrero** is the author of *A Tongue in the Mouth of the Dying* and the forthcoming *A Crown for Gumecindo*. Her honors include an Alfredo Cisneros del Moral Award, and an International Latino Book Award.

Timothy Liu's most recent book is *Don't Go Back To Sleep*. New work appears in *American Poetry Review* and *The Awl*. He lives in Manhattan with his husband.

Éireann Lorsung runs Dickinson House and MIEL. Two collections are out from Milkweed Editions. Now she is working on a novel about archives and earthquakes.

M.C. Mah is a critic and novelist with work in *The Nervous Breakdown*, *KGB Lit Mag*, *Full Stop*, and *The Rumpus*. He lives in Brooklyn.

Mariana McDonald's work has appeared in numerous publications, including poetry in *Anthology of Southern Poets: Georgia* and fiction in *UpDo: Flash Fiction by Women Writers* and *So to Speak*.

Jen(nifer Wilson) McGuire is a writer and actor living in NYC. She is at work on a collection of essays and a novel about jealousy in the digital age.

Joseph Mills holds an endowed chair, the Susan Burress Wall Distinguished Professorship in the Humanities, at the University of North Carolina. He has published five poetry collections with Press 53.

Laura Jean Moore's poetry, essays, and stories have been featured or are forthcoming in *[PANK]*, *Corium*, and *Change Seven*. She holds an MFA from Columbia University and a BA from Reed College.

Natasha Murdock is working on an MFA in poetry at Arizona State. She lives in Gilbert, AZ, with her tiny family. You can find her most recent poems in *So to Speak* and *Four Chambers Magazine*.

Liza Porter's chapbook *Red Stain* was published by Finishing Line Press in 2014. She received the 2009 Mary Ann Campau Memorial Poetry Fellowship from the University of Arizona Poetry Center.

Colin Rafferty lives in Richmond, Virginia, and teaches nonfiction writing at the University of Mary Washington. He is at work on a collection of short essays about the presidents.

Lee Ann Roripaugh is the author of *Dandarians*, *On the Cusp of a Dangerous Year*, *Year of the Snake*, and *Beyond Heart Mountain*. She is editor-in-chief of *South Dakota Review*.

Susan Rukeyser writes because she can't stop. Believe it, she's tried. *Not on Fire, Only Dying* finally found its perfect home with Twisted Road Publications. It debuts in fall of 2015

Michael Salcman was chair of neurosurgery at University of Maryland and president of the Contemporary Museum. His books include the collections *The Clock Made of Confetti* and *The Enemy of Good is Better*.

Olvard Smith grew up in Hawthorne, California, a city rich in the comic despair and urban flavor that serves as the primary impetus for his stories. He is an MFA fiction candidate at Rutgers-Newark.

Nikki Thompson is a poet and book artist (Deconstructed Artichoke Press). With an MFA from California College of the Arts, her work has appeared in *Palimpsest*, *Mason's Road*, and other journals.

Vickie Vértiz has written for the *Los Angeles Review of Books* and with McSweeney's and the Poetry Foundation. She's writing a memoir called, *Smart: Growing Up Gifted and Brown in Southeast Los Angeles*.

D. Watkins is an author, filmmaker and native Baltimorean who graduated with honors from Johns Hopkins University. His work can be seen in *Niche Literary Magazine*, *Welter* and *The Huffington Post*.

Tom Williams is the author of *Don't Start Me Talkin'* and *The Mimic's Own Voice*. He also contributed to *Four Fathers* and *Daddy Cool*. Williams is the English department chair at Morehead State University.

Sarah Ann Winn's poems will appear soon in *[d]ecember*, *Massachusetts Review*, *Quarterly West*, and *RHINO*, among others. Her chapbook is called *Portage* (Sundress, Winter 2014).

2014-2015 Cobalt Press Titles

Four Fathers: poetry and fiction ($15)
Dave Housley, BL Pawelek, Ben Tanzer, Tom Williams

Black Krim: a novella ($15)
Kate Wyer

How We Bury Our Dead: poetry ($14, due February 2015)
Jonathan Travelstead

A Horse Made of Fire: poetry ($14, due August 2015)
Heather Bell

Additional 2015 titles to be announced.

For more information about Cobalt Press publications, including our quarterly and annual literary journals, visit www.cobaltreview.com/cobalt-press.

www.ingramcontent.com/pod-product-compliance
Lightning Source LLC
Chambersburg PA
CBHW070321190726
48291CB00014B/2529

* 9 7 8 1 9 4 1 4 6 2 0 5 8 *